Gould

SUPPORTING EARLY
LITERACY
DEVELOPMENT

Exploring best practice for 2-3 year olds

Featherstone
An imprint of Bloomsbury Publishing Plc

50 Bedford Square
London
WC1B 3DP
UK

www.bloomsbury.com

FEATHERSTONE and the Feather logo are trademarks of Bloomsbury Publishing Plc

First published in Great Britain 2017

A catalogue record for this book is available from the British Library.

ISBN
PB: 978-1-4729-4588-4
ePDF: 978-1-4729-4587-7

2 4 6 8 10 9 7 5 3 1

Printed and bound in India by Replika Press Pvt. Ltd.

This book is produced using paper that is made from wood grown in managed, sustainable forests. It is natural,
renewable and recyclable. The logging and manufacturing processes conform to the environmental regulations of
the country of origin.

To find out more about our authors and books visit www.bloomsbury.com. Here you will find extracts, author
interviews, details of forthcoming events and the option to sign up for our newsletters.

The author wishes to thank children and staff from Evergreen Day Nursery Swinton Manchester, TTS,
Beehive Nursery Manchester and COSY of Derby for giving permission to share images in this publication.

Contents

Introduction

With recent increased levels of accountability across the world of education, and two-year-olds now becoming an established part of the school population in some areas, it is critically important that those working with some of our youngest children (whether they be in a nursery, a children's centre, a school or with a child minder) fully understand how literacy can be successfully approached at this sensitive, early stage of their development. There has never before been a greater number of two-year-olds accessing funded places in early years provision than there is now.

Whenever the conversation turns to the subject of emerging literacy, we need to consider exactly what 'literacy' is, and how it manifests itself through and in our youngest children. Literacy is about communication and, for very young children, can be defined as being 'about communication in all its forms':

- listening
- speaking/signing
- reading
- writing.

Literacy is continually evolving for very young children. It begins from birth, through children's interactions with others and the environment in which they live, learn and move. This evolution continues through their experiences, as they are exposed to a literate world: an environment of books, magazines, comics, newspapers, signs and notices.

While the sequence of literacy development follows the same general pattern, individual rates of growth often vary. It is therefore most important to understand where a child is stage-wise (rather than age-wise) so that the next steps for them can then be carefully planned and progress can be maximised.

Defining literacy may or may not be controversial, but how we deliver and best support its development with very young children certainly can be. That literacy development is important should not be in question, for it is literacy that will help to define our children as they grow and develop into adulthood.

The Ofsted *Common Inspection Framework*, launched in September 2015, has established the need for further improved levels of teaching, learning and assessment so that even more of our young children achieve a good level of development (GLD) at the end of their time in Reception. The overall vision that is now firmly established is that all children, including (significantly) those from the most deprived backgrounds, must be given the best possible start in the Early Years Foundation Stage (EYFS) to take forward into their lifelong learning journey.

The EYFS profile results, published as national data at the end of the Reception year, continue to show that not only is literacy at the lowest level of attainment of all of the seven areas of learning, but it is also within this area that the gender gap nationally is the widest of all. There is a 10 percent gap in reading and a 13 percent gap in writing between girls and boys (DfE, 2016). This data also shows that 76.8 percent of girls achieved a GLD in reading compared to only 62.1 percent of boys; this a gap of 14.7 percent (DfE, 2016).

When Nicky Morgan was Education Secretary, she highlighted the importance of curriculum areas such as literacy in her speech, *When knowledge matters* (2015), stating that 'Our schools have the greatest responsibility of any of our civic institutions. They help to shape the next generation – the generation that will decide Britain's place in the 21st century, the generation that will write the next chapter in our island's history'. This quotation engages with the importance of literacy competence in helping to raise the aspirations of the next generation of children in Britain, whatever their social background.

Children's early achievements in literacy are often key to their later progress at school. Hence, some key questions are raised around early literacy, such as:

- How can we best support children to develop as early stage readers and writers?

- How can we provide stage-appropriate opportunities that will inspire all children to want to and be able to become literate from an early age?

- How can we ensure there is sufficient emphasis on suitable progression and continuity in literacy?

- How can we, as a nation, narrow the wide gap in literacy attainment between boys and girls?

- How can we support our very young, disadvantaged children to progress as early readers and writers and so positively shape their future life expectations?

This book does not advocate the formal teaching of reading to younger and younger children, but rather it emphasises:

- the nurturing of skills such as the enjoyment of books in a more natural way

- the promotion and support of skills across the learning environment provided

- the critical role of literacy-rich play and active learning experiences

- the importance of positive interactions between young children and adults around literacy.

This book has been written for anyone interested in the development of young children. It is for teachers, early years practitioners, students, parents and carers and for all those interested in working with two-year-olds in the future, or managing those who work with two-year-olds in whichever kind of provision.

Chapter 1

Young children and their developing literacy competencies

> *It's not just about what we provide for children, but also how we support them in their interactions.*
>
> **Terry Gould**

Early literacy development is a continuous developmental process that begins in the first years of life, but children first need to be inspired to gain a love and hunger for engaging with literacy. Early literacy skills develop through and in real life scenarios and settings as a result of positive interactions with literacy-linked materials and other people. A key concept to be recognised is that language, reading and writing skills develop at the same time and are intimately linked.

What do we know about the literacy development stage of children who are two years old?

Here are some examples of what you might hear someone say on the subject:

- Two-year-olds sometimes generalise about concepts, e.g. an apple is a ball or all four-legged animals are dogs.

- Many use the words 'me' and 'mine' quite a lot.

- They seem to use that word 'no' very frequently.

- Some enjoy imitating and mimicking.

- A high proportion of two-year-olds like to repeat favourite nursery rhymes and simple songs.

We could go on drawing out what a two-year-old might do or say or be like. However, the difficulty is that not all two-year-olds are like this or that – they are not all exactly the same. They like to do, say, listen to or play with/around different things. So it's dangerous to generalise too much. However, we do need, through observation, to consider what stage of literacy development a child is at as a starting point so as to be able to plan the next steps in their learning. We need to support them by ensuring that we meet their identified needs and know their starting points. This cannot be achieved unless we closely observe children and then use these observations to make informed judgements about what they need next.

Children will often mark make, draw and write using whatever implements they can find.

Where children's development follows a more standard pattern, they:

- have greatly increased their skills in communication from being a one-year-old
- are able to hold higher levels of conversation, and show an interest in language – including an increased vocabulary.

Hence, as early years practitioners, parents or carers, we should together think of two-year-old and three-year-old children in terms of:

- what they do/can do
- what they are interested in/like to do
- what they need in terms of experience
- their level of language and communication development
- the stage of their current early reading and writing development
- their attitude/disposition towards early reading and writing
- their developing understanding of the reading and writing process and its purpose.

Then, based on this, we should provide a shared ethos of approach, together with a range of practical ideas which can be used to support improved developmental outcomes.

Early language and literacy skills development

The development of early language and literacy skills – speaking, listening, reading and writing – is very closely linked to:

- children's earliest experiences with books, stories, signs and notices
- the interactions that young children have with literacy materials such as books, paper, pencils, crayons and other mark making materials
- the interactions children have with the significant adults in their lives and how these interactions inspire them to further engage.

One of my frequent assertions is that core subjects like literacy and mathematics are all around us – an idea which has itself been around for some time.

When a child creates with blocks, when he communicates with paint, when he uses his body freely as a means of expression, he is being taught to read.

Dell H. Hymes, 1963

This statement by Hymes underlines the point that every learning environment, whether it be the construction area, the creative workshop or the book area, can have the potential to support early literacy. It raises the fundamental point that early literacy does not just take place in the book area or the mark making area but in all areas of the setting and the wider environment.

Developing early literacy for very young children doesn't just involve books or other literacy-based materials, but also skilled and knowledgeable people (practitioners, parents, carers) who develop sensitive, responsive relationships with the children, and can use these and their knowledge of the children to gently guide them towards becoming competently literate. Practitioners, parents and other caregivers are thus a vital component of an individual child's experience with reading and writing.

There are of course many variables along the way:

- the child (their needs, interests and starting points)

- the books/printed reading materials available

- the quality of the accessible 'learning' environment

- the range and variety of opportunities to speak, listen and learn language

- the range and quality of the mark making/writing tools and mediums

- the skills and knowledge of the parent, carers and practitioners

- the relationships adults and other children have with the child.

Each of the above are needed and must coexist in harmony – together they will support the development of emerging literacy skills.

Successful early literacy support does not mean formally teaching reading or writing to infants and toddlers. Toddlers who feel pushed to read may become frustrated or fearful and begin to associate these negative feelings with books – potentially impacting negatively on their future confidence, interest and joy in books and language. It's important, therefore, to have suitable stage-appropriate quality books readily available for them to engage with and for adults to 'bring to life'.

How do reading and writing skills evolve?

Reading and writing will evolve from a number of early, stage-appropriate skills, e.g.

- physically manipulating or handling books

- looking at and recognising books

- interpreting pictures and babbling in imitation of reading

- modelling with malleable mediums such as dough and clay

- making marks with a range of mark making tools on mediums such as paper, white boards, flagged areas or large wall boards.

Very young children at the 16–26 months stage will make marks for a wide variety of reasons, each of which will have its own validity as they test the hypotheses they have about the world around them. As these children move along their journey of mark making through the 22–36 months towards the 30–50 months stage, they will begin to learn to recognise the difference between drawing and writing. Practitioners and parents must ensure that they value and celebrate children's mark making, including supporting a sense of achievement and self-esteem. This is because there is a recognised dynamic relationship between achievement and self-esteem that in itself greatly supports increased levels of motivation and concentration.

Children often seek out natural materials to explore mark making – in this case mud and a stick.

Within this relationship, strategies should be utilised that support children's awareness of languages and writing systems other than that of English, as well as other communication systems such as Braille, Signalong™ or Makaton™, so as to encourage a breadth and inclusivity of approach. Some children may write from right to left, such as those whose first language is Arabic and whose experience at home is of this language. These children's home languages must always be valued as highly as English as they develop as bilingual or multilingual learners.

As children can learn such a lot from the world around them, we should aim to give all our young children a wide-ranging breadth and variety of experiences with people, places and things. This will provide a better chance when they start to read texts; these texts will be that much more meaningful because of the early engagements as the ideas and concepts in the texts will be more familiar.

When children engage with their environment, e.g. going to the shops or a garden centre, visiting bus and train stations or taking walks in the countryside, they have the opportunity to see new and different things, and through this, extend their vocabulary and communication skills as they talk about their experiences. Children who have had these experiences in great measure learn to make sense of the story better and more quickly than those who don't. In fact, many EYFS providers make group

big books with their children about the trips they have done. In these big books, they include what the children have said about their experiences, e.g. 'We fed the baby goats' underneath a picture of the children feeding the baby goats. These books can then be placed in the book area for children to independently engage with.

Book behaviours

Very young children exhibit book behaviours when they engage with books. These behaviours can be generically summarised under four headings:

1. Book handling

2. Picture reading

3. Story and book comprehension

4. Story reading.

1   Book handling

Book handling refers particularly to children's physical manipulation. These physical behaviours are the result of the interaction between the pages and content of the book they are handling and their own characteristics (which are influenced by their stage of development, their interests and their previous experiences). Hence the importance of making the right kind of good quality, stage-appropriate books, both story and non-fiction, available to them. For many two-year-olds, 'lift-the-flap' books can be very engaging, as can those with bright and attractive pictures and with interesting content; the lift the flap book *Dear Zoo* by Rod Campbell springs to mind.

2   Picture reading

The behaviours associated with this aspect of literacy describe the ways in which children interact with the pictures in the book. They will often point to the pictures and say what they see, or use the pictures to tell or retell the story involving the characters and events. Good quality pictures are invaluable for engaging children's interests, even when they cannot yet read the text. Pictures are useful for all children, but even more so for learners with English as an Additional Language (EAL). For EAL children, picture reading enables them to think in their home language and to then use this in their talk. It is also of great value where members of staff are able to speak in the child's home language. The pictures can be supported by dual language text. Although the very young child may not able to read the text yet, they often do know that this is, for example, Arabic or Urdu writing as opposed to English. Seeing their home language in books can reinforce that their home language is valued.

3 Story and book comprehension

Very young children can demonstrate in a variety of ways that they understand what a book is or may be about. They may laugh or smile at a picture or select a book based on its content. For example, they might pick up a book about farm animals after playing with small world farm animals. Alternatively, they may home in on their favourite page of a book by searching for it.

Later, after engaging with a book, they may perform an action that was shown in the book such as throwing a ball or pretending to feed a dog. They may make associations between books so that after choosing to engage with one book about bears, they then select another book about bears.

When we set up a book area, we learn that children engage with books that bit better when it is a small and cosy space rather than one which is large and exposed. We also need to think carefully about how we store the books we provide for children and whether or not all the books are matched to the children's stage of development and their identified interests.

4 Story reading

These behaviours refer to what children verbalise in their interactions with the book or text. They may read to a puppet or stuffed toy or say part of the text immediately after the page is turned. They will sometimes recite part or whole phrases from favourite stories or fill in the next part of the story after listening to the adult reading. They may talk about the characters and events in storybooks in ways that indicate that they have understood what has been said or read. When an adult misreads a word or phrase that is familiar to them as part of a story, they will challenge this and can typically offer the correct version.

As they progress their skills as beginner readers, they may also move their finger or hand across a line of text and say what they think it says or even make attempts to read very familiar books for themselves, particularly when the storyline is quite predictable. They may also relate the book to their own experiences.

Author's Note

The next chapter will look in more detail at the influence of the environment and how it can impact on outcomes relating to children's literacy development.

Chapter 2

Exploring the importance and main elements of a literate environment

> *We need to focus on the range and the quality of what we provide.*
>
> **Terry Gould**

It is the range and quality of literacy-linked *experiences* that children have that help to maximise their potential in terms of the *skills* and *knowledge* they then acquire. Over time, this leads them on to a secure but ever growing level of *understanding*.

In facilitating and supporting these experiences, we should always keep at the forefront of our minds that the following three key aspects underpin all that we do with young children, including when supporting their early literacy development:

- **Relationships** – how we respond to and engage with children.

- **Environment** – providing the right type of experiences for children through a high quality indoor and outdoor learning environment.

- **Vision** – how we plan the way forward, including the next steps in what we provide for two- and three-year-olds.

We can use these three aspects to self-evaluate significant aspects of the literacy journey upon which we are taking our children.

Children learn from everything they do. The quality and range of the experiences they are presented with, both in the setting they attend and at home, are critically important to their achievements. There will be a significant difference in the skills and knowledge already achieved between two- and three-year-old children who have had a wide range of stimulating experiences at a setting and at home

and those who, for whatever reason, have had limited or very few such experiences. The GLD levels assessed by teachers at the end of the EYFS in the Reception class will reflect this enormously. Hence, we all need to recognise that the earlier we provide the right kind of experiences for young children, the more we are supporting them to engage with and develop their early but growing literacy skills.

There is a need to aim to continuously improve outcomes in literacy for *all* children, within the EYFS and beyond. All very young children need to be surrounded by adults who are able to make their literacy learning journey a rich, plentiful and meaningful one. To succeed in this goal, there is a need for the adults to facilitate, provide and suitably maintain an active, play-based learning environment; one in which children are immersed in literacy and which skillfully supports and fosters each of the three characteristics of effective teaching and learning (COETL) identified in the *Statutory Framework for the Early Years Foundation Stage* (DfE, 2017). These are:

- **playing and exploring** – children investigate and experience things, and 'have a go'.

- **active learning** – children concentrate and keep on trying if they encounter difficulties, and enjoy achievements.

- **creating and thinking critically** – children have and develop their own ideas, make links between ideas, and develop strategies for doing things.

> *A quality learning experience for children requires a quality workforce. A well-qualified, skilled staff strongly increases the potential of any individual setting to deliver the best possible outcomes for children.*
>
> **DfE, 2017**

Suitably trained, enthusiastic and experienced adults are a key part of the environment that we provide for young children. We need to remember this when we are appointing new staff or providing coaching or training to existing staff. The quality of EYFS staff is so important, as without them, learning will not happen as it should. Knowledgeable adults will help to ensure that the key aspects of a suitably rich literacy environment for two- and three-year-olds is in place, such as providing a wide range and variety of the mark making and early writing opportunities through which children are enabled to record their ideas graphically, as well as a range of suitable stage-appropriate fiction and non-fiction books.

It is only when children begin to realise that marks can be used to carry meaning in a similar way to spoken words that they can then begin to use these marks as a tool to represent their thinking in visible and meaningful ways. Children need to be supported to learn that text carries meaning and can be read again and again. Spoken and written language are the child's first encounter with symbolic representation as they slowly begin to learn how communication works. There are some parallels to be drawn between the development of early language and mark making/writing. A stimulating literate environment supports this growing awareness.

Literacy development opportunities should be available to children every day in every developed 'workshop-type' area they can access, e.g. the construction area, small world area, creative area. This means taking up and developing an ethos which supports the idea that books are not only to be found in a 'book area', but also across and around the learning environment, including in the outdoor space. The same applies to mark making/writing. This should be facilitated not only in the mark making or writing areas, but in and across the whole learning environment, including that outdoors. Children will only be able to reach their potential in an environment which makes it possible for them to do so.

Within all of this, there needs to be careful thought given to creating a suitable balance between adult-led and child-initiated learning opportunities. Part of this will be as a result of an ethos that promotes daily interaction with books (both fiction and non-fiction), signs throughout the setting and e-games and activities, including:

- a visual timetable

- story and non-fiction books

- displays

- signs and notices

- easy-to-use computer programmes

- labels on toys and resource boxes (picture and written word)

- song and rhyme cards

- name cards used to support self-registration (signing in)

- writing frameworks.

All providers must regularly, as a team, review the routine of the session or the day the children attend and through this reflect on the balance of adult-led and child-initiated learning. Within this, they can then plan to employ innovative strategies and projects that support literacy, particularly in the adult-led parts of the session.

Cosy book areas outdoors can attract children to engage with books.

Innovative Literacy Strategies

Foundations of Literacy superbly focuses on the following seven strands of practice:

1. **Learning to listen**

2. **Talking skills**

3. **Music movement and memory**

4. **Storytime**

5. **Learning about print**

6. **Tuning into sound**

7. **Motor control.**

FOUNDATIONS OF LITERACY
by Sue Palmer and Ros Bayley (revised edition, 2013)

1. Learning to listen

This is about children becoming able to discriminate between sounds, e.g. between foreground sounds and background noise. This will include discrimination between a widening range of sounds, e.g. a fire engine siren and a phone ringing. They will develop their aural attention span as well as their social listening skills, including making eye contact and attending to the speaker. Later, there can be a focus on mental imaging through their auditory memory.

2. Talking skills

Talking skills can compensate for language delay by including expansion and 'pole-bridging' talk. It is also about social speech skills, including awareness of audience and turn-taking. Vocabulary will be developed and extended through explaining, exploring, planning, predicting, recalling, reporting and analysing.

3. Music, movement and memory

This is about children developing a sense of rhythm, beginning with the ability to hold a steady beat. Music and movement can help to develop the speech and listening skills mentioned above, especially articulation, voice control and turn-taking through singing in time with others. This is also about the development of auditory memory; physical coordination and motor control and left-right brain interaction.

4. Storytime

Storytime develops the speech and listening skills in 1 and 2, especially social skills and auditory memory. It also promotes familiarity with written language patterns, story grammar and prediction skills.

5. Learning about print

Awareness of the nature and functions of print are foundations of literacy. Knowledge of the alphabet letters and concepts of reading and writing facilitate emergent reading and writing. Knowledge of essential sight words promotes confidence.

6. Tuning into sound

This is about children's listening skills and general language awareness including their awareness of rhyme, rhythm and alliteration (phonological awareness); blending and segmenting (phonemic awareness); and the alphabet code (phonic knowledge).

7. Motor control

Refinement of motor control from large scale to fine control and hand-eye coordination is important for letter shape formation; development of the finger muscles; and pencil grip and control.

Two-a-day stories with two-year-olds and three-a-day stories with three-year-olds

One strategy that I have found to be highly effective is to implement what I call 'three-a-day stories with three-year-olds' and 'two-a-day stories with two-year-olds'. This is an innovative idea adapted from one first put forward in *Foundations of Literacy* (revised edition, 2013).

Let me take an example of this in practice to bring the idea to life for you. In a pre-school room of a day nursery, with 20 three year old children attending for most sessions across the week, the room leader purchased 20 high-quality storybooks. These included the following:

- *The Pig in the Pond* by Martin Waddell

- *Gecko's Echo* by Lucy Rowland and Natasha Rimmington

- *Dear Zoo* by Rod Campbell

- *I Don't Want Curly Hair!* by Laura Ellen Anderson

- *A Beginner's Guide to Bearspotting* by Michelle Robinson and David Roberts

- *Little Rabbit Foo Foo* by Michael Rosen

- *Up, Up and Away* by Tom McLaughlin

He then placed green tape down the outside spine of each book to show these were the special books for the project and kept them in a very attractive, linen-lined wicker basket on an accessible shelf. He talked to the children about the books and how the new project was going to work. He also sent home a letter to parents explaining this and identifying the books they were using. He had already been to the local library and they had ensured that at least two copies of each book would be on their shelves for loan. He explained to parents in a meeting, followed up with a letter, that they could borrow these books from the local library if they wanted to.

On the first day, the practitioner chose three books to read to the children at one of the circle/group time sessions. He repeated this using the same books on day two and also on day three. Then on day four he changed one of the books, putting the book he was replacing into the listening area. Each day after this, he changed another book, then another book, until he had read each of the twenty books to the children. He then started again by adding the first book back in, and so on. To help him remember the order, he wrote them down on a list, which he laminated and placed into the wicker basket with the books. Over a period of time, he monitored the impact of the project. It was clear that a significantly higher number of children than in previous years were achieving the *Development Matters* statements around reading in the 22-36 months, 30-50 months and even in the 40-60 months sections. Children were achieving in much larger numbers and much earlier.

Monitoring of any such project in this way is critically important because it allows you to know and accurately report what is working well and also to identify ways to further improve what you do. The manager of the nursery sat in on some of the sessions and discussed her observations with practitioners in the room. She felt that the project could be further improved by using some of the children's home languages of Somali, Urdu and Polish. As they could not get all the books they wanted in dual language from the publishers, they adapted some of the books themselves, adding laminated printed text to the pages to include the same text in these home languages as well as English. They spoke with the library service and they agreed to obtain the texts where possible in dual languages and add these to their stock for loan.

The project clearly made an positive impact on the outcomes for those children. The nursery is now looking further into their data to see if there are any significant differences in outcomes between boys and girls in reading and, if so, how they can positively address this.

They are also shortly going to be rolling out 'two-a-day stories with two-year-olds' in their toddler room, which has 16 children attending for most sessions. So they are looking to purchase 16 stage-appropriate high quality storybooks, including several 'lift-the-flap' type books. Working in the same way as the pre-school room, they will be reading two stories each day and changing these until they have read all the stories, then starting again and working through the list in the same order that they started.

Song and rhyme cards

Another useful idea to consider implementing is the use of song and rhyme cards. One easy way of creating these is to use software such as PowerPoint™ and A4 sized paper. The chosen song or rhyme, e.g. *Five Little Speckled Frogs*, can then be printed out on one side, folded in half and laminated. Photocopies should be made before lamination so that you are ready to let parents have a copy to use with their child at home once children are learning these. When several song and rhyme cards have been made (a minimum of three or four), these can then be used with the children.

One way of using song and rhyme cards is to lay several of them (four-six works well) picture side up on the floor in front of the children at circle/group time and ask a child to choose one. An age-appropriate discussion can then take place with the group as to what they think the song or rhyme is about. Then the song or rhyme can be sung or

Five Little Speckled Frogs

Five little speckled frogs sat on a Speckled log eating the most Delicious grubs yum yum.

One jumped into the pool where it was nice and cool then their was four green speckled frogs glub glub.

Four, three, two

One little speckled frog sat on sat on a speckled log eating the most Delicious grubs yum yum. He jumped into the pool where it was nice and cool then there were no green speckled frogs glub glub.

Five Little Speckled Frogs

chanted by the adult and the children. Over time, the children's song and rhyme repertoire will grow as a result and their language skills will also grow. Songs and rhymes with linked actions are often particularly enjoyable. You can produce song and rhyme cards in English but also in other languages, such as children's home languages.

Performing songs and rhymes outdoors

Just as we need to provide children with a range of literacy-linked learning opportunities indoors, we also need to do so outdoors (but often on a bigger scale). The best way to support performing songs and  rhymes outdoors is to set up a 'performing arts' area in your outdoor provision where children can recite or sing familiar songs and rhymes. This can be as simple as making a platform from an old wooden pallet with the top and sides filled in and a non-slip surfacing added to the top, such as artificial grass. Add to this some resource boxes of dressing up materials, including wigs, show business-style glasses and a simple echo-type microphone. The song and rhyme cards created indoors can then be used outdoors by children who can select what they are going to perform either individually or in a small group.

Starting with a story

This is yet another idea that starts with a laminated sheet. This time, make a colour photocopy of a the front cover of a storybook and laminate it. Cut the page into four or more pieces (subject to the stage of development of the children) and then place the pieces around the outdoor area for children to find. Once the pieces have been collected, help the children to put the pieces together and discuss what the story could be about.

The next day, or later that same day, place artefacts relating to the story around the outside area in small drawstring sacks (or a suitable alternative) for the children to find. The children should bring the bags to the group and open them together to create a collection. Discuss the items in relation to the cover – do the items help reveal more of the story?

To complete the initiative, the next day produce the actual storybook and read it to the children. As the ideas unfold, more able and older children can then be encouraged to create their own spin-off stories such as the same story but with a different ending or with another character added.

By using ideas, activities and strategies like those mentioned in this chapter, you will support children in many ways. You will see this by looking at the in *Development Matters* statements, e.g. at 22–36 months, a child:

- has some favourite stories, rhymes, songs poems or jingles

- repeats words or phrases from familiar stories

- fills in the missing word or phrase in known rhyme, story or game, e.g. 'Humpty Dumpty sat on a…'. (*Development Matters*, p28)

As children move through to the 30–50 stage (and remember that in the EYFS it is about stages not ages), they will be further supported to also:

- Enjoy rhyming and rhythmic activities

- Show an awareness of rhyme and alliteration

- Recognise rhythm in spoken words

- Listen to and join in with stories and poems, one-to-one and also in small groups

- Join in with repeated refrains and anticipate key events and phrases in rhymes and stories

- Begin to be aware of the way stories are structured

- Suggest how the story might end

- Listen to stories with increasing attention and recall

- Describe main story settings, events and principal characters

- Show interest in illustrations and print in books and print in the environment

- Look at books independently

- Handle books carefully

- Know information can be relayed in the form of print

- Hold books the correct way up and turn pages

- Know that print carries meaning and, in English, is read from left to right and top to bottom. (*Development Matters*, p29)

For those children who are advanced for their age, they may also demonstrate some of the aspects outlined for the 40–60 months age group. These children may:

- Enjoy an increasing range of books

- Know that information can be retrieved from books and computers

- Continue a rhyming string

- Link sounds to letters

- Begin to read words and simple sentences. (*Development Matters*, p29)

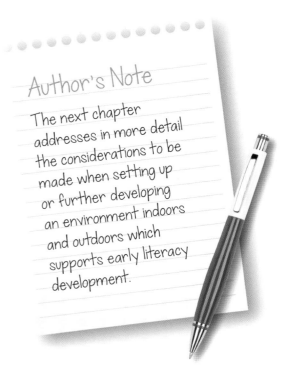

Author's Note

The next chapter addresses in more detail the considerations to be made when setting up or further developing an environment indoors and outdoors which supports early literacy development.

Chapter 3

Creating an environment that supports literacy

> Environments speak to children, so we need to inspire them through what we provide.
>
> **Terry Gould**

The importance of the learning environment cannot be overstated. To revisit the beginning of chapter 2 (page 12), "It is the range and quality of the literacy-linked *experiences* that children have that help to maximise their potential in terms of the *skills* and *knowledge* they then acquire". Hence, we need to create an environment that provides such a range and quality of experiences.

There are, for me, four key factors that underpin an effective literacy-linked learning environment indoors or outdoors.

- **Time** – how long children can and do spend in these areas in concentrated play and learning. In many ways, this will be determined by the nature of the area and the routine of the day or session.

- **Space** – the size and development of the space and how it is set up and used.

- **Easily accessible resources** – children need to easily access a suitable range and variety of resources to support, facilitate and develop their interests and learning needs.

- **Emotional wellbeing** – when children's emotional wellbeing is really well supported by the environment, they are much more likely to make better progress. A cosy book area will be more inviting to a child because it is more emotionally supportive.

All of this will be underpinned by the way adults support children, including interacting with them and observing them, and then planning the next steps for them.

Setting up and developing the environment indoors and outdoors

When setting up or developing an **indoor environment** that supports literacy, you will need to think about:

- the routine of the day
- access to the outdoor area
- which areas to include indoors
- positioning of the areas
- size of the areas
- resourcing of the areas (linked to available funding)
- staffing levels
- lighting
- ease of access to resources for children
- where the opportunities are which will support literacy outcomes
- the views of children and their parents or carers
- the role of the adult.

For the **outdoor environment**, you will need to think about:

- the routine of the day

- access to the indoor area and toilets

- which areas to include outdoors

- positioning of the areas

- size of the areas

- resourcing of the areas (linked to available funding)

- creating and using outdoor resource boxes

- maintenance implications

- staffing levels

- ease of access to resources for children

- where the opportunities are which will support literacy outcomes on a bigger, bolder, messier and noisier scale

- the views of children and their parents or carers

- the role of the adult.

Offering the children a wide range of experiences is important to their language development.

Both **indoors and outdoors**, all practitioners will need to:

- facilitate opportunities which support early literacy development, including scaffolding learning through the effective use of the practitioners

- challenge children with new opportunities which build on existing skills and knowledge

- enhance on a regular basis what is offered for children to initiate their own learning, and in this way, promote and support child-initiated learning

- plan stimulating and exciting experiences which inspire interest and engagement

- provide positive feedback to children

- interact with children

- extend and develop children's language, communication and thinking skills

- ensure the outdoor area is safe, secure and hazard free whilst remaining challenging

- act as a good role model

- respond to children's interests, patterns of behaviour and cultural diversity.

Adults will, as a part of this, need to employ strategies that support and complement the environment they have created, some of which should include:

- open-ended questioning
- modelling thinking out loud
- suggesting
- recapping
- showing interest in children's ideas and their engagement with literacy
- respecting children's own decisions and choices
- tuning in to what is being said and done by children
- clarifying thinking

- reminding
- sharing their own experiences
- offering alternative ideas/thinking
- encouraging further/more elaborate thinking
- recasting children's talk
- following up children's interests.

All of these strategies should be underpinned by quality observations. Below is an example of how this type of practice can take place.

SPIDERS AT OUR NURSERY

This case study serves as an excellent example to demonstrate how many of the strategies previously mentioned can be closely linked.

At a Salford nursery setting, outdoors in early November, the children were excited to see that there were spiders building a web on one of the bushes. The adult tuned into this interest and began to watch quietly alongside the children. She asked the children open-ended questions such as how long they thought the spiders would be there and how big the web might be at the end. She modelled her thinking, suggesting what type of spider it might be and how they might make their own webs later using wool. She suggested they bring a camera outside to take photos of the spiders and the web.

The children agreed, and several really good images were recorded. The interest of children was maintained by the spiders until it was time to go indoors for circle/group time. The adult used a big book about spiders at the gathering time to engage the children, who were able to talk at length about what they had seen that morning.

The next day, five of the best photos were printed out and, with the children, the practitioners made a book entitled *Spiders at our nursery*. The text for the book was developed through the practitioner asking the children open-ended questions about the photos and their experience watching the spiders, with her acting as scribe to note down what they said. Once completed, the book was then read to the children and placed in the book area for children to share with each other. It proved very popular with all children, but particularly those who had watched the spiders the previous day.

The opportunities taken up by the adult were:

- recapping the experience
- open-ended questioning
- modelling thinking out loud
- tuning in to what is being said and done
- clarifying thinking and encouraging further and more elaborate thinking
- following up children's interests.

Setting up and developing workshop-type areas

Indoors

In the two-year-old room, sometimes called the 'Toddler room', and the three-year-old room, often called the 'Pre-school room', the environment is best created by developing the space into workshop-type areas, such as: the book area, the construction area, the writing/drawing area or the mark making area, and the creative workshop area. Further advice on creating workshop-type areas can be found in *Learning and Playing Indoors* (Gould, 2012).

Each of these developed areas can offer a substantial range of experiences that will support and promote early literacy. Early writing, mark making and drawing should not be confined to the writing/drawing area but supported across all areas. The same is true for reading; this should not be confined to the book area but provided across all other areas.

Creating and developing workshop areas enables children to engage in structured ways with early literacy both through adult-led and child-initiated activity.

Outdoors

So long as there is suitable space, the outdoor environment should reflect the learning and development needs of the children, including early literacy development, but in bigger, bolder messier and noisier ways than indoors. The outdoor areas for two-year-olds and three-year-olds can be divided into zones, which are the outside equivalent of workshop-type areas. Within these areas, offer a variety of learning opportunities, including those which support literacy.

These zones could include some of the following, as identified in *Effective Practice in Outdoor Learning* (Gould, 2011) and *Learning and Playing Outdoors* (Gould, 2013) but what you can offer will very much depend on the space available:

- roadway
- running and ball play
- climbing and adventure
- digging
- planting and growing
- natural
- wildlife
- natural materials, e.g. sand, water, etc.
- creative modelling
- sitting/reading/gathering
- sensory
- imaginative play
- minibeasts
- construction and building
- performing arts.

What would an environment that supports literacy development in an EYFS setting look like in practice?

The following opportunities would be provided for:

- Children able to display and celebrate each other's mark making, e.g. through a 'wow wall' or another form of display of their work.

- A wide range of materials and resources which children can freely engage with both indoors and outdoors, including jumbo chalks and paintbrushes.

- A range of 'writing frameworks' which children can add to in the role play area, the construction area and the writing/drawing area.

- Engaging with print, including that in books and signs reflecting some different languages which are significant to any of the children.

- Support to further develop their vocabulary and then use it in their play and other activities.

Practitioners would continuously self-evaluate the range and quality of the opportunities which they offer in the learning environment with deep self-questioning, such as:

- Is there a sufficient range of opportunities for children to get deeply involved in sustained ways?

- Is there sufficient inspiration to motivate children to attempt to mark make or write and engage with books?

- Are there quiet spaces where children can engage in reflective play as well as larger spaces where they can test out their gross motor skills?

- Are there suitable gathering spaces where children can engage in group or circle time activities with the adult?

Monitoring is most important here. Below are some self-evaluation questions you might use to monitor and evaluate the environment your provision is offering:

- Does the environment inspire children to engage with it?

- Do you provide space and time for them to engage?

- Is it bright and vibrant?

- Is it clear to children how they might use the space?

- Is it continuously being suitably enhanced?

- Is it appropriately maintained?

- Does it make children want to be there?

- Do parents and carers think it is special and exciting for their child?

- Is it impacting on outcomes within the area of literacy and those areas closely linked to this?

Resources to support mark making and early writing

Indoor resources

These might include:

- clipboards, paper and pencils, including 'talking clipboards'

- dance music – making marks to music and using ribbons on sticks to make marks in the air

- phones and notepads, diaries, appointment book, pens and pencils to record messages, e.g. in role play

- clay or dough and simple tools

- music-making area, including support for symbolically recording notes

- stampers and ink pads

- mini whiteboards and marker pens

- a variety of envelopes, paper, postcards greeting cards, pens and pencils.

Outdoor resources

These might include:

- chunky chalks

- fabric sheets with mud and different sizes and lengths of sticks

- forest area or suitable alternative – for making marks with sticks in the mud

- water spray bottles for spray painting

- clipboards and paper and pencils, including 'talking clipboards'

- collections of containers for squirting or pouring

- builders' trays with different textures for mark making

- wall boards lined with paper and rollers, paint or water

- paper rolled out on the floor with brushes, stampers and other tools/ implements.

Author's Note

It has already been identified that the role of the adult carries key importance as it impacts on enhanced outcomes. The next chapter takes this idea forward.

Chapter 4

A closer look at the role of the adult

The kinds of roles adults adopt make a real difference to children's literacy development.

Terry Gould

The role of any adult in supporting literacy development, whether this is an EYFS practitioner or a parent or carer, is of critical importance. This is because children start to learn about reading and writing before they start learning to read and write. Children start learning about reading when they see others they know reading, and they start to learn about writing when they see those familiar to them engaging in writing. They take this forward by watching others and then having a go themselves.

Writing and reading for different purposes

The adults around children, both in settings and in the home, introduce children to ideas about writing and reading for different purposes. This often includes cereal and other food packaging, greetings cards, street names and bus, airport and railway timetables as well as stories, non-fiction information texts, songs and rhymes. Parents and carers need to be supported in their understanding of this by staff in the setting their child attends so that they feel empowered to help their child at home as much as they possibly can.

The young child wants to do what the adult does and wants to be able to do 'the real thing' – in the same way as they want to help with the shopping, decorating, baking or washing up. Using what they know, the young child makes efforts to read or write like the adult, reflecting what they already know about reading and writing.

If adults provide children with simple pencil and paper type resources, such as old diaries or notebooks, two- and three-year-olds will imitate the function of writing long before they can manage to produce conventional letter forms. They will 'pretend' write what they know the adults close to them write, whether this be shopping lists, the nursery register, phone messages, letters, stories, recipes, filling in forms, etc.

If we visit libraries and provide children with suitable age-appropriate texts of fiction and non-fiction, they will 'pretend' read, and in this way show us what they understand about the processes involved. Nowhere is there more potential for them to do this than in the role play or imaginative play area – indoors or outdoors. When set up well, role play is a very powerful support for literacy, as the case study on page 27 demonstrates.

CHILD'S EYE MEDIA CASE STUDY

Child's Eye Media commissioned a short research project at a Manchester based primary school into the benefits of role play on communication, language and literacy outcomes for nursery-aged children.

The project used DVDs, a range of role play outfits and a number of writing frameworks to support the children to develop their skills. Nursery staff reported that the seven-week project had a positive impact both on the professional practice of staff and, significantly, on the outcomes for children. Additionally, the project had positive results in the staff's work with parents.

When the initiative began, most children were working within the 22-36 months age band of the EYFS *Development Matters*. By the end of the seven weeks, almost all were working securely within the 30-50 months band in all communication, language and literacy scales.

Literate Role Play Provision

Inspired by detailed scenes in the DVDs of a vet's surgery, a fire station and a post office, three irresistible role play areas were created each featuring a display of carefully labelled photographs, signs and notices.

Mind maps were created with the children before and after each theme was introduced, and were useful indicators of pre- and post-theme development. They revealed that children's understanding of the roles of vets, firefighters and postal workers had increased, together with their vocabulary, use of expressive language and extended sentences.

Sufficient props were provided so as not to overwhelm the children but to encourage sharing and careful handling. Children took pride in wearing the outfits – some even thought that they couldn't be a firefighter, vet or postal worker unless they wore the outfit!

Writing props were part of the provision. For example, the vet's surgery had its own reception desk with writing framework sheets, a telephone and pencils.

Home-school Links

The project proved very successful in involving parents in their children's learning. A talk was given to parents at the start of the project to explain its purpose. Parents were offered the opportunity to loan the DVD to watch with their child at home and many took this up. One parent who worked at the post office visited the nursery to talk with the children.

Author's Notes (Terry Gould)

This research shows how much carefully planned, structured and well-delivered role play can impact on improved outcomes for children, particularly in the areas of communication, language and literacy. However, it can also support all seven areas of learning and development as well as the three characteristics of learning, and has other potential spin offs such as within the parent partnership area.

Those working with two- to three-year-olds are advised to carefully reflect on the quality and impact of role play provided both indoors and outdoors as this is one of the key ways that children's progress can be suitably supported and encouraged.

Sharing reading and modelling language

In the early stages of reading, children need the support of age-appropriate, high quality texts (fiction and non-fiction) with lots of pictures and images that inform them about the writing. They also need interested adults who spend quality time sharing, reading and talking about the texts with them. Children love to hear favourite stories many times; through this they come to understand:

- the structure of the story

- what a character is

- that stories have beginnings and endings

- that written print can be read exactly the same time after time

- that literacy is a fun thing to engage with.

Every sharing of a book, whether this be a piece of non-fiction, e.g. about cars or the sea, or a storybook, is an opportunity to support literacy through language development at all stages of a young child's development.

When sharing a book alongside a child on a one-to-one basis, it is important to model language. Adults should interact with the child where they can and use descriptive commentary – talking about what they or the child is seeing or hearing. During these interactions, modelling language and using descriptive commentary should be used far more than direct questioning of the child. When asking questions, adults should always allow a suitable lengths of time – thinking time – for the child to formulate responses, particularly with very young children, those with developmental language needs and sometimes with children where English is not their first language (EAL).

Meeting the Ofsted requirements

To meet the 'outstanding' criteria set by Ofsted in the area of outcomes for children, providers must ensure evidence of the following:

> - *Children make consistently high rates of progress in relation to their starting points and are extremely well prepared for the next stage of their education.*
>
> - *Almost all children in the provision, including disabled children, those who have special educational needs, those for whom the setting receives additional funding and the most able, are making substantial and sustained progress that leads to outstanding achievement.*
>
> - *Gaps between the attainment of groups of children in the setting, including those for whom the setting receives additional funding, have closed or are closing rapidly. Any differences between outcomes in different areas of learning are closing.*
>
> - *Children are highly motivated and very eager to join in. They consistently demonstrate the characteristics of effective learning.*
>
> **Early Years Inspection Handbook, Ofsted, 2015**

These criteria will not be met in a setting where the environment fails to meet the needs of the children or within a provision where the role of the adult is not one which inspires children, keeps them safe and maximises their progress in all areas, including literacy.

Within any EYFS provision, the adults are expected to provide an exciting and stimulating environment that supports all seven areas of learning and development. To ensure that the adults are suitably able to plan for children's learning, there is a requirement that they observe children and, where an observation is significant, consider recording this. From such recorded observations and what they already know about the child, practitioners should then assess the child's development stage

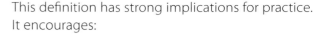
and identify the next steps for them in their learning and development. If children are not making the expected progress, then adults need to review what is happening and consider the use of intervention techniques to support the child.

What is required as part of the current Ofsted *Common Inspection Framework* (2015) for the inspection of EYFS provision, is that:

> *ALL children make good or better progress based on their identified needs and their starting points.*
>
> **Ofsted, 2015**

This includes the area of early literacy. Ofsted have produced a definition, which states that teaching and learning is to be defined through the following:

> *Teaching should not be taken to imply a 'top down' or formal way of working. It is a broad term that covers the many different ways in which adults help young children learn. It includes their interactions with children during planned and child-initiated play and activities: communicating and modelling language, showing, explaining, demonstrating, exploring ideas, encouraging, questioning, recalling, providing a narrative for what they are doing, facilitating and setting challenges. It takes account of the equipment adults provide and the attention given to the physical environment, as well as the structure and routines of the day that establish expectations. Integral to teaching is how practitioners assess what children know, understand and can do, as well as taking account of their interests and dispositions to learn (characteristics of effective learning), and how practitioners use this information to plan children's next steps in learning and monitor their progress.*
>
> **Early Years Inspection Handbook, Ofsted, 2015**

This definition has strong implications for practice. It encourages:

- a high quality learning environment indoors and outdoors

- systems for effective observation recording and assessment for learning

- effective but manageable planning which demonstrates support outcomes for all children

- teaching which inspires children to engage and make suitable progress

- knowledgeable, effective and supportive practitioners

- a strong partnership with parents which impacts on outcomes for children.

So, all adults working in EYFS settings must work to:

- create an environment which supports children's learning and development

- spend suitable amounts of time interacting with children to promote creative and critical thinking skills and early language and communication

- encourage parents and carers to become more involved in their child's development

- give ideas as to how parents and carers can support this development at home

- identify as early as possible any additional needs a child may have and strengthen links with colleagues, such as health visitors, who can support these needs.

Key areas of literacy skill for adults to focus on

There is a saying that if you don't know what you should be focusing on, then its very likely that you will not focus on what you should. This is definitely true in the EYFS. There are six key areas of early literacy skills within which adults need to support the young child. Knowing about these and then deciding, as a team, how best to implement them is most important – I include parents in this team.

1. Print motivation

Instilling in children the joy of and interest in reading. Adults need to keep reading and sharing books in a fun way at home and at the provision. Fun is so important – if the experience is not a positive one, children can begin to relate reading to something negative which may make them less likely to choose to read.

2. Narrative skills

Retelling stories and events and adding descriptions. The ability to describe things and events, and the ability to tell stories, helps children better understand what they read.

3. Print awareness

Children knowing that print has meaning as well as how to handle a book and recognising print in the environment. Being familiar with printed language helps children feel comfortable with books and understand that print is useful.

4. Letter knowledge

Children knowing that letters are different from each other. Children learn that the same letter can look different and that each letter has a name and relates to a specific sound.

5. Phonological awareness

The ability to hear and play with the smaller sounds in words. This includes rhyming, breaking words apart and putting word chunks together, and hearing beginning sounds.

6. Vocabulary

Knowing the names of things and understanding the meaning of words. The more words young children know before they join the Reception class at school, the better. Children who have never encountered a word will have a hard time reading it in a book later on. All experiences children have can further support and develop their vocabulary.

How might we support and deliver these for our children?

1 Print motivation

- Model the fun of reading and of playing with language – enjoy the book and the interaction and help children to enjoy reading.

- Keep children involved when reading to and with them.

- Say the words of big books together in chorus.

- Use non-fiction books such as poetry and information books too.

- Have children (and adults) join in during appropriate parts of the story.

- Have a comfortable 'book area' for children and adults to share reading time together.

2 Narrative skills

- Take time before or during storytime to talk about an unfamiliar word.

- Retell stories with puppets, a flannel board, props, or creative dramatics.

- Help children expand their descriptions of things.

- Ask children to describe their drawings, or to tell a story about them.

- Ask children to make predictions about a story.

- Engage in a two-a-day and three-a-day story initiative (see Chapter 2, pages 15-16).

3 Print awareness

- Run your finger under a title or repeated phrases.

- Write out songs and rhymes on flip charts or posters.

- Read books with print as part of the text.

- Talk about environmental print, e.g. road signs, menus, food labels.

- Start with a book facing upside down and play the clown, asking which is the right way up?

- Use name tags and allow children to have a go at writing their own name tag.

- Point out different kinds of print within books.

4 Letter knowledge

- Help toddlers to see and feel different shapes.

- Point out letters and words on toys, food boxes and other objects.

- Play matching games to spot what is alike and what is different.

- Have children make letters with fingers, bodies, clay, paint, etc.

- Use name tags, ideally some made by the children.

- Have magnetic, foam and material letters available to 'play' with.

5 Phonological awareness

- Point out rhyming words in books.

- Play with a particular word from a story: what rhymes, what words start with the same sound, etc.

- Sing songs and repeat them.

- Change the initial sound in familiar songs, or a repeated phrase in a story.

- Play with 'nonsense' or silly words.

- Play word games.

- Use song and rhyme cards (see Chapter 2, page 17).

6 Vocabulary

- Take time before or during the reading of a book to explain an unfamiliar word (don't replace the word).

- Take time before or during the reading of a book to talk about a word's other meanings.

- Take time before or during the reading of a book to add descriptive words.

- Use non-fiction that offers new words.

- After reading a book, go back to an interesting picture and talk about it, using less familiar words.

- See whether toddlers can point to, pick up and name familiar objects – use real items when possible, e.g. spoon, apple, doll, etc.

Opportunities that support literacy in the developed learning environment

You should consider where the opportunities are within both your indoor and outdoor environments for children to mark make or write and engage with books and signs or notices, etc. You should consider how you can help them to maximise their development as early mark makers/writers and readers as a result.

Firstly, think about your two-year olds. What are they likely to be interested in and able to be doing at this stage of their development?

Then, think about your three-year-old pre-school children and what they are likely to be interested in and doing at this stage of their development.

Finally, think about what they need to learn and how you can blend this in with their interests and abilities.

Ideas for two-year-olds

Maybe your two-year-old grips the pencil or crayon or other writing implement in the palm of their hand (palmar grip) and makes lots of seemingly random marks or scribbles. Perhaps they make marks that overlap or are layered by repeated 'over marking/writing'. They may pick up a book and handle it badly or with growing skills. They may share the book with another child, an adult or a puppet and try to tell the story.

Whatever the children do, your role is to observe and then respond. This starts with practitioners showing an interest in children's mark making, early writing and their engagement with books, and then planning how to respond and take things forward together with parents.

Things you might do:

- Join in with the play and imitate the marks the child is making.

- Reinforce the fact that some surfaces can be written on whilst others are not appropriate, e.g. not on a chair but on paper, etc.

- Provide a range of mark making and early writing materials such as large sheets of paper, some in different colours, and a wide range of writing implements.

- Give them the opportunity and the freedom to make marks in other ways, such as in shaving foam in a builders' tray, in paint with cards, in sand or in food, such as custard or semolina.

- Share books on a daily basis such as through two-a-day stories (see Chapter 2, pages 15-16); encourage parents to use the local library or even set up a storybook loan service from your setting.

- Let the child see you, as the adult, mark making and writing.

Ideas for three-year-olds

Later, as the child develops as an emerging writer, often around the age of two and a half to three-years-old, they will begin to alter how they hold the writing implement, moving from a palmar grip to a pincer grip. This is a significant move forward as it signals a greater level of maturity as a writer and the ability to engage with more control in the writing process.

It is likely at this stage that the child will progress from making random marks to a more determined effort to create some separate symbols. They will attempt to close shapes, making an inside and an outside, combine lines and shapes and explore separate but also linked shapes. Practitioners should continue to observe what children do and then respond to this.

Responding to a child really starts with showing an interest in their mark making/early writing, giving positive feedback and then planning how to respond and take things forward.

Things you might do:

- Join in with a child's activity and imitate what or how the child is writing.

- Reinforce again that some surfaces should not be written on and make clear which ones can be used.

- Model writing and the writing implement grip for the child. This continues to be important.

- Model using different writing materials such as pencils, crayons, felt-tips, chalk and boards, clipboards and paper – again model the grip as you do so, ensuring that this is firm and effective.

- Talk with the child about what they or you have written or drawn.

- Let the child see you writing.

- Point out the child's name and other print in the learning environment.

- Continue to provide free access to a wide range and variety of resources and materials that the child considers interesting. These resources should provide open-ended opportunities for the child to mark make and write using a range of implements both indoors and outdoors.

- Provide early writing opportunities through role play and the use of writing frameworks.

- Start to make the link for children between what is said and what is written – although this can begin at this early stage, it may take some time for the child to fully grasp this concept.

Modelling

Modelling has come up in this chapter quite a few times. We need to model in lots of ways how children might do things, and watch to see how they copy what we do!

Modelled writing should:

- happen daily or at least frequently

- be cross-curricular

- happen in all developed areas of the learning environment, e.g. the role play area

- happen at group time and during adult-focused and targeted activities, as appropriate

- be short and simple – sometimes just one word.

Modelling is particularly useful with three-year-olds but remember it is stage not age in the EYFS.

Literacy-linked activity in different areas of your setting

There is potential for a great deal of literacy-linked activity to take place in the different areas or zones of your setting. The following lists are not prescriptive or final but merely give some starting points to enable an adult to feel they can and will move forward in what they provide. Several areas have been focused on for further insight.

Literacy links in the book area

- Encourage children to look at and handle books with developing care, e.g. turning pages carefully from front to back.

- Include stage-appropriate books, e.g. those with lift-the-flap features, large pictures, less text.

- Encourage children to talk about characters and events in books.

- Children could draw aspects of a familiar or favourite story, using clipboards, paper and pencil from the writing to go box.

- Working with an adult, children could put four or five pictures from a familiar story in the correct sequence and talk about them.

- Create silhouettes of the books and ask children to put books back onto a matching silhouette.

- Create an interactive display linked to a particular book in or close to the book area. Include props for children to act out and talk about the story.

- Include stories with large images and matching puppets, e.g. *Giraffes Can't Dance*.

- Include story sacks.

- Include rhyme sacks and boxes.

- Provide puppets.

- Hang a selection of words attractively displayed in the area.

- Include a child's family book.

- Tell or read a story to children using props and different voices.

- Include books made with the children.

Literacy links in the mark making, drawing, writing area

- Include lots of books to write and draw in, e.g. old diaries, exercise books, notepads, etc.

- Provide mini chalkboards and chalk. Include mini whiteboards and washable marker pens.

- Include small clipboards and pencils.

- Provide simple writing frameworks.

- Model writing, e.g. model writing a poem or some messages.

- Include a writing easel.

- Have a fixed whiteboard or wallboard available for the children's use.

- Include a selection of catalogues linked to the children's interests for them to cut out.

- Display an alphabet line.

- Include a display of writing or drawings the children have produced.

Literacy links in the creative workshop area

- Encourage children to make an attempt at writing their own name on any piece of paper, piece of work or model produced.

- Encourage children to find their own name from a collection and glue this onto the bottom or top part of a picture.

- Depending on their stage, children could mix their own paints from 22-36 months.

- Provide catalogues and other materials for children to cut out from and glue onto paper to make collages.

- Include small rollers that make different shaped and different sized paint marks for the children to explore.

- Invite children to help you make dough and then allow them to explore the dough – excellent for finger and hand muscle development.

- With adult support, as required, the children could make a label for a model.

- Include opportunities for finger and hand painting.

- Include shaving foam (or suitable alternative) in builders' trays to explore this using fingers or small sticks.

- Introduce golf balls, cars or marbles for mark making in paint.

- Include opportunities for hand or foot printing.

- Include a selection of different 'tools' to explore, e.g. tongs, tools, tweezers, sponges, etc.

- Include opportunities to explore leaves and natural materials, e.g. spaghetti letters.

- Have a selection of paper, plastic, card or wooden letters.

Literacy links in the role play area (or child-initiated imaginary play supported by adults out of this area)

- Include a range of opportunities and equipment for children to use for writing, e.g. notepads and pencils for leaving phone messages; creating signs and labels.

- Encourage the reading of signs provided, e.g. 'open', 'closed', 'exit', 'entrance', 'Special offer', 'for sale', etc.

- Include a selection of linked books for reading or looking at.

- Children could play out a story – either real or imaginary.

- Encourage using real resources, e.g. handling money, using office equipment, exploring real food.

- Encourage stage-appropriate reading and writing opportunities to match the chosen theme, such as:

  - opening times, price lists, order forms, catalogues of stock, cheques or gift cards for a shop

  - appointment cards, appointment books and phone message books for a vets

  - menu boards, recipes, bills for a café

  - tickets and booking forms for a travel agents

  - appointment or weight cards for a baby clinic

  - eye test card for an opticians

  - estate agents sheets

  - instructions for use, e.g. for toys in a toyshop or seed packet instructions in a garden centre

  - letters and labels for parcels in a post office

  - directions in a tourist office

  - staff or visitor signing in sheets for a toy factory or airport

  - customer comment book or complaints book for a hotel.

Literacy links in the water and sand areas

- Leave a message in a bottle.

- Bury treasure and ask the children to mark on a map where it is.

- Create opportunities for children to play with buried or floating letters.

- Encourage children to play with letters written on small plastic balls (e.g. on table tennis balls).

- Create letters or words in ice.

- Include resources for children to play out nursery rhymes, e.g. five ducks for *Five little ducks*.

Literacy links with the routine of the day

- Provide images of the daily routine with matched writing, e.g. 'story time' with a picture of a storybook.

- Include adult-led daily stories, e.g. two-a-day or three-a-day (see Chapter 2, pages 15-16).

- Encourage children to find their name and picture laminated card on arrival and at the end of the day.

- Share song and rhyme cards with parents (see Chapter 2, page 17) and add props.

- Develop shared notes to home, e.g. 'Dear Mummy/Daddy/Grandma, etc. Today I played in the book area. I read the book *Gecko's Echo*.'

Literacy links in the fine motor area

- Provide opportunities for children to cut along and around patterns and pictures.

- Provide beads and pasta for threading and pattern making.

- Encourage children to pick up items using tweezers, small tongs or spoons.

- Include magnetic letters and boards.

- Set up a post box.

- Provide play dough and candles.

- Include some locks and keys.

Literacy links with technology

- Use simple cameras with the children to take pictures of them in action and make these into books. The children could make their own or with adult support, as appropriate for the stage, e.g. the adult writes what children say about the pictures. The books can then go into the indoor book area.

- Include a simple remote control car and encourage children to send it to specific points or people following signs or words, e.g. 'under the bridge' – with a picture of a bridge; 'to Majid' – with a picture of Majid.

- Children make themed homemade books with an adult, e.g. 'Where's Teddy?'.

- For older or more able children, include access to stage-appropriate software programmes, e.g. *Mouse in the House*.

- Include simple hand-held metal detectors and encourage children to 'bury' some 'treasure' and create a map for other children to follow to find the treasure. For more ideas see *Press It, Switch It, Turn It, Move It!* (Gould, 2013).

- Older or more able children could write a dance.

Literacy links in the outdoor areas or zones

Mark making and early writing

- Include water pots and brushes for making magic marks – writing and drawing.

- Provide spray bottles, e.g. washing up liquid bottles and other types of squirters.

- Mount a selection of wall or fence mounted chalkboards or whiteboards.

- Mount a selection of wall or fence mounted large-scale painting boards with 25mm and 50mm brushes.

- Include some mud in builders' trays for making marks with sticks.

- Have a selection of jumbo chalks for children to use on the floor.

- Encourage making treasure maps in pirate play.

- Encourage creating and playing with potato dough.

- With older two-year-olds, you could encourage them to play with clay.

Reading

- Set up a treasure hunt in which children dig in a large outdoor sandpit to find some of the letters in their own name or parts of the laminated front page of book.

- Have an outdoor book and reading den.

- Include outdoor signs and labels, e.g. 'this way in', 'open', 'closed' in an outdoor role play area – see below.

- Create an outdoor role play area or role play boxes with emerging literacy opportunities, e.g. a garage or fire station.

- Hold storytime sessions outdoors, both planned and spontaneous. (See Chapter 2, page 18).

- Set up a find the letter game.

Summary of the key aspects of the adult role in supporting early literacy

- Emphasise the value, interest and importance of books.

- Answer children's questions about writing.

- Model mark making and writing.

- Mark make and write alongside children in the learning environment.

- Support the development of the necessary motor skills for writing.

- Observe children's attempts at writing and identify their understanding of writing.

- Observe children's attempts at reading and identify their understanding of reading.

- Consolidate early writing opportunities.

- Consolidate early reading opportunities.

- Keep developing those important partnerships with parents to develop their understanding and gain their support in working at home with their children and supporting what you do in your setting for and with them.

Author's Note

Drawing has been briefly mentioned in preceding chapters. The next chapter focuses on the key role drawing can have on literacy development with young children.

Chapter 5

Drawing and its key role in supporting early literacy development

> *Children should have the opportunity to express in writing and drawing what they have experienced, what they know about and what they can do, what they are interested in or what they are concerned or anxious about. These topics empower children.*
>
> **Diane Rich, 2002**

This chapter will focus on the value of children's drawing in supporting their early literacy. We will consider why we should be fostering and supporting this even more than we may do currently.

The role of drawing in children's learning appears to me to be frequently misunderstood by many EYFS practitioners. Within the EYFS, the opportunity to draw is often freely available but mainly with an adult focus on mark making leading to writing rather than communication and creativity. Yet drawing is one of the many languages children use to communicate about their world, both to themselves and to others. Through drawing, children can represent action, emotion, ideas or experiences.

Until relatively recently, the study of children's drawings has reflected a 'top down' approach which takes the pursuit of realistic representation as its goal. A more modern approach sees things differently; the guidance *Mark Making Matters* (2008), talks about mark making, creativity and critical thinking. One case study in it explains that Louis, as a result of being encouraged to draw, 'is developing his own ideas as he draws and he expresses them as he does so.' In another case study with a childminder, it discusses a child who 'started to draw on the chalkboard outside. As he continued to draw, he talked about his party and began to make a list of the people he wanted to invite'.

This demonstrates the value of encouraging children to draw as its sets the scene for them to share their experiences of their world and has the potential, as in this case, to lead into literacy activity such as making a list.

What young children draw is very much influenced by the context of their experiences, their current thinking and opportunities, and the previous opportunities they have had, along with the support for them to develop their physical drawing skills. As 21st century early years practitioners, we are probably well aware of the modernist thinking that sees the child as a co-constructor of meaning and an active player in his or her world. But we are probably equally aware, as part of the community that we live in, that culture and a child's background act as mediators between the child and his or her environment; the role of adults and more able peers or siblings is significant in 'scaffolding' learning. What their peers are doing is also significant in a young child's learning.

When a child makes an intentional action to create a drawing, then what he or she chooses to draw focuses attention on what they (the child) see as both of interest and emotional concern to them.

Vygotsky (1995) has argued that for the young child, there is a close relationship between play and art and '*the entire process through which children develop cultural awareness*.'

Children frequently draw pictures and tell a story at the same time; they act a role and create their lines as they go along. On most occasions when very young children draw, they rarely spend a long time completing each piece but they do appear to focus all their emotions and attention on what they are doing at that moment in time. Drawing can be seen as a narrative in a child's development. If speech is seen to be internalised as thought, we can surely justifiably assert that drawing is a form of 'graphic speech' that has its own internal visual narrative.

The child uses drawing in an attempt to order and explain the world from all aspects of their experience. It is an action which does not confine them to the spoken or written word and, as a result, they can often draw much in advance of what they can verbalise. As practitioners, we need to consider how we can best enable young children to represent through drawing that which is visually, verbally or kinaesthetically based and is important to them. If drawing is such a liberating thing that helps to free children's thinking, then why would we not encourage it? For example, the child in the earlier case study who started by drawing on the outdoor chalkboard used the freedom it gave him to think and organise his thoughts. Without this experience or opportunity, he may never have decided to think about his party which in turn led him to making a list of who to invite.

Most adults rarely seem to start their thinking with drawing because adult communication naturally relies so heavily on spoken and written language, but this does not mean that children should do the same. Drawings are a natural part of children's communication and, as such, can only help to broaden the child's expressive capabilities. When we reflect on how we as adults communicate, we often use drawings to clarify our thinking but rarely start with them; they come somewhere further along the process. If we want to build an extension to our house, we decide by communication with others (architect, local authority, etc.) in writing or by talk how we will go ahead; only then are visual layouts produced to fine-tune the plans. Children should be encouraged to draw as a way of thinking about and sharing their ideas. As such, drawing *is* communication which is, in turn, all of what literacy itself is about.

There appears to me to be a lack of recognition by many currently working in the EYFS of the power of drawing in serving a narrative function for children by externalizing their experiences, thoughts and feelings. For me, drawing is so powerful because it enables children to express their individual stories which, as yet, they cannot write down. It offers a developmentally-appropriate form of communication and provides a focus for talking about their ideas.

Given the emphasis on reading and writing within the *Statutory Framework for the Early Years Foundation Stage* (DfE, 2017), maybe we, as practitioners and parents, do need to think more out of the box and support the need for a broader view of literacy, one that includes more of an emphasis on drawing – as this is clearly something through which the young child displays a fundamental disposition towards meaning making. If we support children to draw more, this will help to show us more about what they know about the world.

This interesting thought made me dig down into my own personal experiences as an EYFS practitioner in a community nursery centre in Salford many years ago, and remember a particular boy who could draw submarines.

THE THREE-YEAR-OLD BOY WHO DREW SUBMARINES

I had a three-year-old boy in my setting who showed, after several months with us, that he had become able to draw the most amazing and detailed drawings of submarines. It was as if he had somehow managed to get inside the thought processes of the brain of the great Leonardo Da Vinci, who was drawing his ideas for underwater ships many centuries ago. This child's drawings, which were to me quite amazing for his age, all happened because he was encouraged to draw both at home and at the centre. Once he had completed his drawings, he was able to explain at great length (for a three-year-old) how submarines worked. However, his parents were unable to explain how he first got interested in submarines, as he hadn't any books at home and they didn't recall him looking at such books elsewhere. This was something that we were never able to find the root of, in the home or in the setting.

Some staff went to the local library and the main booksellers and bought several books on submarines, which were his clear favourite of all the books we had. He would take them home at night and bring them back the next day so that before long the whole group became knowledgeable about submarines. He wanted to be an explorer when he grew up, but I worried about him; although we fostered this interest and all the literacy it brought him in contact with, how would he do at school the next year as baseline assessment didn't address these skills? I even discussed it with our very experienced local early years adviser.

We didn't have an EYFS then and the curriculum was devised by the local authority, which of course had no mention in it of submarines! The early years adviser told me not to worry, that it would all come out in the wash and that he would do well at school, but I wasn't so sure. He was also fantastic at making clay models of submarines, and of lots of other things too, including animals.

I never got to find out how he did at school as I moved to another local authority, but I do know we supported him. I only wish I had documented and published his work as a case study of the power of drawing and creativity. My question to you, the readers, is what would you do if you had a child like that boy in your setting? How would you support him and how would you ensure his interests and needs were met? Perhaps there is such a child in your setting but no one has really noticed him or her yet, or even worse, he or she will never get to where the boy who drew submarines got to because his or her talents are hidden by not being encouraged to draw.

A closer look at 'scribbling'

By the age of two, most children (but not necessarily all) will have had some experience of using pencils, crayons and felt-tipped pens. Many of these children will still be 'scribbling' and may not produce anything that is recognisable for quite some time. It is unfortunate that many early years practitioners appear to regard scribbling in a negative way. There is more to it than some seem to recognise, and it is a shame to dismiss it as 'just scribbling'.

The benefits of scribbling

- Scribbling appears to be an enjoyable activity for the child, mainly because of the rhythmic movement of the arm involved.

- There are certainly developmental stages in the scribbling process, from tentative stabs at the paper to freer movements which over time become even more controlled.

- This growing control leads eventually to the child being able to produce an irregularly-shaped figure bearing simple resemblance to a circle or an oval. This enclosed type of shape is significant as it opens up possibilities of representation: by placing dots or lines either inside or outside this shape, the child can begin to represent important spatial relationships between objects, figures and living things or parts of these, e.g. a figure's eyes, nose and mouth can be contained within the boundary of the face.

The early part of drawing is scribbling...

Types of scribble

Rhoda Kellogg (1970) wrote about having discovered what she saw as twenty different basic types of scribbles used by young children, including dots, single vertical lines, single horizontal lines, single curved lines, mulitple vertical lines, zigzag and wavy lines, spiral lines, multiple loop lines, imperfect circles, etc. She indicated from her research that few would use all of these at any one time but that some are combined to produce more complicated works. Her claim was that most (but not necessarily all) children go through progressive stages of scribbling.

Not everyone agrees with her about the variety of types of scribble she described. The only agreement seems to be that there are two main types of scribble (Golomb, 1981):

1. **circular loopy or include whirls**

2. **single or repeated parallel lines.**

What we are talking about here is children's spontaneous drawing. The fact that children choose to draw without anyone asking them to do so, provided the materials are there for them to access freely, shows that there is something innate in drawing that they may enjoy doing and which they see as purposeful for them. There are no rules for the young child who freely scribbles. He or she sometimes seeks adult approval of their work, but this may simply be part of their desire for affirmation of their being, rather than seeking a comment on what they produce.

Facilitating scribbling

In the early stages of them becoming writers, children need to develop some control of the tool they are using for mark making or writing as they scribble away. It is through this scribble that they learn how to make marks by pushing, pulling and varying the pressure they use. In this way, they develop the ability to draw the straight and curved marks which they will later use in their drawing and writing. To help children to build up their knowledge of writing tools, adults should facilitate them using different kinds of crayons, felt-tips, pencils and pens and different sizes and textures of paper and card. Adults should allow them plenty of time to experiment with different ways of making marks, as well as encouraging them to become interested in why and when the adults in their lives write.

What can we observe from a scribble?

When we observe children scribble and/or draw, we can notice things such as:

- how long they spend on the activity

- which hand they use

- how they hold the mark making or drawing tool

- the shapes and patterns they choose to use in their drawing or scribble.

These observations are important because they can help the practitioner to support and describe the child's motivation and concentration, as well as their levels of skill in their use of drawing and mark making tools. Children who show no inclination to scribble or draw may be indicating their lack of interest in mark making and perhaps later on in writing. In the same way, scribbling and drawing may be indicators of a child who is predisposed to mark making or early writing.

The question then is, how much notice should we pay to the scribbling and the drawing that comes from our children? If we don't value this and don't support and encourage it, we may be unknowingly discouraging our children from engaging in mark

making and early writing later on. It is important to stress that viewing drawing as a pre-writing skill possibly undermines the complexity and richness of young children's drawings that often belies their apparent simplicity. However, drawing does help to develop the muscle abilities and some of the skills needed to be a writer. Drawing is not then a temporary holding form of symbolic representation leading to the higher-level ability to form letters and numbers, but rather the practice of it does support the physical skills required for writing letters and numbers.

Drawing appears to only be relevant to some of the seven areas of the EYFS educational programme requirements (DfE, 2017), sometimes referred to as 'the curriculum', such as communication and language, physical development and creative development. However, for two- to three-year-olds, it can actually be linked to all seven areas in some ways. For example, the boy who could draw submarines, mentioned previously (page 42), could have his drawing additionally linked to mathematical development and understanding the world. Perhaps too few of the seven areas give drawing enough status in it own right.

Creativity is often a bridge to cross-curricular learning and drawing can, as we have seen, be cross-curricular. When children are creative and curious, they can come up with answers to the problems that they encounter, e.g. how to keep the block tower they have just built from falling over. Creativity also helps children to become thoughtful, inquisitive, and confident learners later on, when they start school.

One of the most important ways that two- and three-year-olds tune in to their creativity is by experimenting with art-based and art-type materials. As the child picks up that pencil, chunky crayon or charcoal and gets to work, you will note that over time what is produced becomes more controlled and complex. It may be that for very young children, art and early writing skills are one and the same – who at this stage yet knows? At first, it's perhaps just about figuring out what these cool things called pencils, felt-tipped pens and crayons and paints can do. Then children discover the link between their hand holding the implement and the line they made on the page. This is the experience of the power of cause and effect. Imagine how exciting this must be for children who can then begin to make a real 'mark' on the world – a mark that is their own and is unique to them. This leap in thinking is helped along by their new and growing ability to hold things in their hands and fingers. The growing control that children gain over the muscles in their hands then lets them move a marker or paintbrush with purpose and with a goal in mind. The same muscles that they will later use to write!

The stages of drawing for young children

Many people have come up with their own continuum of the stages of drawing for very young children, and it is worth looking at these so that we can recognise progression in children's drawing and how these link into the writing stages. For very young children, there are possibly four main stages of drawing and writing that each child goes through up to the age of around three. Growth doesn't happen at the same speed for every child, but by offering repeated fun experiences with a variety of creative and writing materials, progress over time will happen. For the following stages, remember that it is about stages not ages in EYFS. The ages are given as a very broad guide:

1. **Random scribbling (up to around two years old).**

2. **Controlled scribbling (aged around two to three years old).**

3. **Lines and patterns (aged around three to three and a half years old).**

4. **Pictures of objects or people and linked writing (aged around three and a half to five years old).**

1 Random scribbling

This is the period when young children are just figuring out that their movements result in the lines and scribbles they see on the page. These scribbles are usually the result of large movements from the shoulder, with the crayon, pencil, felt-tip, marker, the wooden stick in the clay or mud, or the paintbrush held in the child's fist. There seems to be joy in creating art at all ages for the child, but at this stage especially, many children relish the feedback they are getting from their senses: the way the crayon feels, the smell of the paint, the squishyness of the clay.

For other children, this sensory information may be too much and they may not enjoy some art activities at this stage (like finger painting). As they grow to tolerate more sensory input, adults can incrementally reintroduce creative and art activities into the routine.

2 Controlled scribbling

At this stage, children develop better control over the muscles in their hands and fingers. Their scribbles begin to change and become more controlled. Toddlers may make repeated marks on the page, e.g. open circles or diagonal, curved, horizontal, or vertical lines. Over time, children begin to make the transition to holding the crayon or marker between their thumb and pointer finger.

3 Lines and patterns

Children are now beginning to understand that writing is made up of lines, curves and repeated patterns. They try to imitate this in their own writing. So while they may not write actual letters, you may see components of letters in their drawing. These might include lines, dots and curves. This is an exciting time as they are realising that their drawing conveys meaning! For example, a child may write something down and then tell you what word it says. This is an important step toward reading and writing.

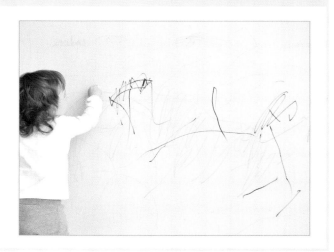

4 Pictures of objects or people and linked writing

Many adults think of 'pictures' as a picture of something. This ability to hold an image in your mind and then represent it on the page is a thinking skill that takes some time to develop. At first, children name their unplanned creations. This means that they finish the picture and then label their masterpiece with the names of people, animals, or objects they are familiar with. This changes over time.

At this stage, it will soon become apparent to you that children are clearly planning prior to drawing what they will create. You will also see more detail in the pictures and more control in the way children handle the crayon or marker, and the use of more colours. What else should we be on the lookout for? Children's first pictures often build off circles. So, you may see a sun (an irregular circle with lots of stick 'rays' shooting out) or a person (usually a circle with roughly recognisable human features).

Once children have begun to purposefully draw images, they have mastered symbolic thinking. This important milestone in thinking skills means that a child understands that lines on paper can be a symbol of something else, like a house, a cat or a person. At this stage, children also begin to understand the difference between pictures and writing. So you may see them draw a picture and then scribble some 'words' underneath to describe what they have drawn or to tell a story. When children are able to share their story with you, they will be motivated to 'author' more and more work as they grow. Children will also begin to add words which they make a good attempt at.

What can practitioners do to encourage drawing and linked writing skills?

- **Rename your writing or mark making areas** to also include drawing, e.g. 'writing and drawing area'.

- **Make creative drawing a regular part of your daily provision** – offer chunky, easy-to-grip crayons, thick pencils and washable markers to draw with. Cut up paper bags to draw on (sometimes it helps young children if you tape the paper down on the table so it doesn't move as they draw), or provide clipboards with paper.

- **Limit your instruction to children** in order to free up their thinking, let the children experiment and explore freely. Creativity means having the power to express yourself in your own way. This independence is just what a growing child is looking for to feel confident, competent and clever. By sitting nearby, observing and giving feedback on the creation, you are providing all the guidance that is needed.

- **Notice the process, not just the product** – we tend to compliment children on their successes, e.g. *What's that a picture of? A house? That's great!* And sometimes we get hung up on the fact that trees should be green, not purple. Sometimes we quiz them, e.g. *What's the name of that colour?* However, children learn more when we don't focus so much on what they are drawing but on what they are thinking and later saying about their drawing. Take a few moments to observe the child at work before maybe commenting, e.g. *Look at the circular lines you are making – there are so many of them!* Or, *That picture is really interesting. Those colours are so bright they make me feel happy!* Or, *I see you are working really hard on your drawing.* Or, *Tell me about your picture.* Then, see if the child is interested in sharing more and go from there.

- **Experiment with a greater variety of art materials** – especially as the child gets more able around the 36 months stage, let children paint with cotton balls, sponges or string; give children crayons to rub over a textured surface (like a coin or a screen); draw with chalk on outdoor surfaces and see how water changes the colour of the chalk when it rains; add powdered paint or glitter to the sand tray, or even add a new dimension to water play by adding drops of washable food coloring or flavouring to the water and let children see what happens when they mix two different colours of water together.

- **Use art to help the child express strong feelings** – if a child is having a tantrum, offer some play dough or set out the markers and paper and suggest he or she makes a very, very angry picture. Creative activities can sometimes help children express and make sense of feelings that are too intense for them to share in words.

- **Encourage the child's attempts to write** – if children scribble something and then tell you what they 'wrote', take it seriously. Let them take their 'shopping list' to the supermarket or mail their scribbled letter to someone. This is how children learn that words are powerful and have meaning.

- **Display children's art and writing** – this is how children know their work is valued and important. Creative activities help children to learn how to solve problems, come up with their own answers, discover the cause and effect of their actions, and feel confident about the choices they make. Art experiences help children to develop independence within limits, and give them the opportunity to represent their ideas on paper or in other formats. Most importantly, creative expression lets children tap into the magic of their own imaginations which is what being a child is all about.

Author's Note

A secure understanding of the stages of development of scribbling and of child development generally are clearly important. The next chapter focuses on the value of understanding child development.

The importance of a secure understanding of child development – exploring a simple writing continuum

Being familiar with the development stages children go through is critical to meeting their needs.

Terry Gould

Child development is one area in which most practitioners think they are highly competent (or at least claim to be) and that there's no need for them to attend any further training. Yet, whenever I conduct training, there seems to be a distinct lack of secure knowledge in this area from a significantly high proportion of delegates. As a result, I feel that when considering literacy, a good place to start is by reviewing child development.

Development Matters in the Early Years Foundation Stage is a non-statutory framework used by many EYFS staff to determine the level of development children are at. This book has aimed to cover the development for those children aged two and three years of age, so mainly covering the 22–36 months and 30–50 months stages. But, as the EYFS is about stages not ages and given that some children are ahead of their chronological development stage and others behind this, we will also be looking at 16–26 months and 40–60 months. However, we should always consider children's individual needs and their starting points.

Child Development SEND and EAL

There are a significant proportion of children who are identified as having special educational needs and/or disabilities (SEND) which impact on their learning and development. Many will not meet their developmental milestones and these children will need additional support to be planned in order to maximise their achievement. Additionally, there are increasing numbers of children starting their early years learning journey for whom English is an additional language (EAL). This latter group of children shouldn't be labelled as having special needs just because English is a second language for them. They may need targeted support but this is not the same as SEND support.

Chapter 6
The importance of a secure understanding of child development:
exploring a simple writing continuum

Statistics indicate that around 17 percent of children currently starting primary school in England have a mother tongue other than English. This figure is constantly increasing and that trend looks set to continue. More than two hundred languages are spoken in the homes of children attending schools in England. We need to celebrate the home language of each of our children. No harm will come to a child's language development if one language is spoken at home and another within the setting, and practitioners should actively promote this practice. If a child can progress and confidently learn one language (their mother tongue), this will mean that the child will have developed secure linguistic skills including knowledge of grammar and sentence structure that will then be transferable in developing and learning another language. Being bilingual is an asset because:

- there are advantages for children's learning

- a strong foundation in their home language will support the acquisition of other languages

- it is vital for maintaining family structure and relationships.

Children need a strong foundation and confidence in their home language and culture to feel confident exploring the language and culture of others.

Bilingualism

There are different types of bilingualism. The typical bilingual language development that we experience with two- and three-year-olds is 'simultaneous bilingualism' which follows this general pattern of stages:

1. **child mixes languages**

2. **child separates languages**

3. **child uses mainly one language.**

As practitioners working with children engaging in this typical bilingual language development, we also need to be aware of the 'sequential bilingualism' stages:

1. **home language use**

2. **non-verbal period**

3. **telegraphic speech**

4. **productive language use**

5. **competent language use.**

It is critically important to explore what home language or languages are used. This is useful in helping to:

- identify if children are having difficulties

- communicate with parents and families

- promote children and families feeling valued, respected and included

- support home language(s) development

- develop positive relationships with children and their families

- support the development of the setting's language.

Chapter 6
The importance of a secure understanding of child development:
exploring a simple writing continuum

Speech or language problems

If a child has a speech or language problem, it will show up in both languages. It won't, however, have been *caused* by the child learning two languages. If you are involved with a child who is learning a second language and you have concerns about speech and language development in their first/home language, then an EAL child may be diagnosed as having SEND needs and as a consequence further support may need to be provided. This further support should be created in consultation with a child's parents or carers, and a plan to meet the child's identified individual needs created. This should involve targets being set, a period of time to cover these, strategies to be used and success criteria so that progress can be evaluated and suitably challenging new targets set.

Ofsted recognises that children identified on the SEND register may not make as much progress as their peers who do not have the same needs. They make it clear through the inspection framework that 'all children should make good or better progress based on their identified needs and starting points' (Ofsted 2015).

The task of practitioners, with the support of parents, is to ensure that whatever children's needs under the SEND framework, and whatever additional needs or challenges the children have, they plan to meet these and make sure the Ofsted criteria on progress are achieved for all children.

Each setting needs to consider how they, alongside parents and carers, can support and extend the language of EAL children, e.g.

- continue to talk even when children do not respond

- persistently include EAL children in small groups with other children

- use varied questions

- include other children as the focus in the conversation

- use the child's first language

- accept non-verbal responses

- praise minimal language effort

- expect children to respond with repeated words

- structure educational programmes to encourage child-to-child interaction

- provide activities which reinforce language practice through role play at all stages – it is important to model language while playing alongside a child

- use descriptive commentary – talking about what you or the child is doing

- modelling language and using descriptive commentary should make up most of your interactions; less should be used on direct questioning

- allow time for children to formulate responses.

Chapter 6
The importance of a secure understanding of child development:
exploring a simple writing continuum

Mark making and early writing continuums

When focusing on child development, a number of people have come up with a variety of mark making and early writing continuums. This simply means they have put together a 'stages of development' framework for this.

One such simple mark making and early writing continuum for two- and three-year-olds might look like this:

1. **Scribbles using a developing grip of the mark making implement (e.g. pencil).**

2. **Scribbles become more patterned and some move from left to right.**

3. **Draws more clearly defined pictures and talks about them.**

4. **Starts to use letters in drawings.**

5. **Uses beginning sounds to communicate about drawings.**

6. **Uses beginning, middle and end sounds to make an attempt to write words.**

When considering the mark making and early writing that children produce, practitioners will need to make some assessments and from these plan the next steps for every child. This is where the mark making and early writing continuum can prove helpful, alongside the observations they make about the child in their activity.

The following are some observations that staff in one nursery in Manchester have made over a period of time about their two- and three-year-olds.

- 'Sahid really seems to enjoy making marks on paper with a range of mediums and tools. He frequently chooses pencil and paper type activities.'

- 'Tammy "writes" mainly in scribble, saying to the practitioner, "This says… ." She makes marks on paper which show an attempt to write.'

- 'Sean can hold and use a writing tool in a developing pincer grip to draw and write his own name.'

- 'Tanzin uses largely unconventional symbols as she makes efforts to write about her picture.'

- 'Mazzine believes he can write. He says about own writing, "This says… ". '

- Mary knows writing is different from drawing and can say which is which. She can identify a picture or drawing and some writing. She often asks an adult what she or he is writing. She is starting to ask an adult to write for her as she creates stories and she draws the pictures of the story.'

- 'Jane can "read" her own marks and writing to others.'

- 'John has experienced creating "shared and scribed" writing with an adult, where the adult writes down what the child says for them.'

- 'Through her experiences of free play with writing and mark making materials, Jean shows an awareness of how writing moves across the page, always making her attempts to write from the left.'

- 'Tommy attempts to write some letters in his own name and he can name these. He can correctly form some letters such as T and O.'

- 'Milly is starting to write using some conventional letter shapes.'

- 'When Adrian makes his attempts at writing, he shows that he knows that there are spaces between words and that he knows about capital/upper case letters and lower case letters.'

Chapter 6
The importance of a secure understanding of child development:
exploring a simple writing continuum

Understanding the developmental stages of mark making and early writing

Understanding the developmental stages of mark making and early writing helps practitioners to monitor learners' growth as writers, identify appropriate teaching focuses, and select teaching approaches to meet different learning needs.

The developmental stages of mark making and early writing are not to be viewed as discrete, sequential stages. Children developing those early skills will demonstrate a range of behaviour, attitudes and skills depending on the complexity of the mark making or writing task and the degree of support provided. Practitioners will need to be aware of possible disparities between the development of some children's early skills and their ability to compose a text. Many children may be able to create texts that are well beyond their ability to write themselves by hand (Gould, 2005), which opens up a number of issues. To help avoid frustration, specific handwriting tasks appropriate to their physical abilities should be planned while children's 'composing' abilities are recognised. Methods of recording their writing, such as adults scribing or using a computer or tape recorder should all be considered. Hill et al. (2006) describe learning to write or to represent language in written symbols as involving learning to use a writing tool, to hold it properly and to create letters, words and sentences to convey meaning to others.

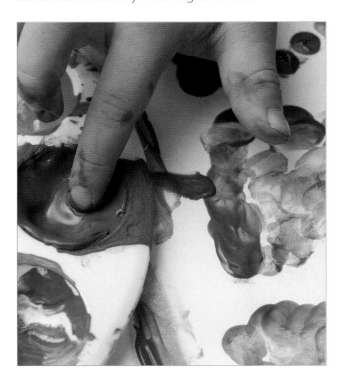

Emergent drawing and writing skills are crucial in the development of handwriting. A child will make marks on paper from an early age and call it 'their writing'. Marie Clay (1991) describes their repetitive squiggles or attempts at adult writing as the 'recurring principle'.

Hand-eye coordination is important in the development of handwriting. Young children should be supported in the development of their hand-eye coordination, balance, spatial awareness, fine and gross motor skills. Children's early ability to grasp and manipulate writing tools will vary depending on their experiences and level of development. When they feel confident, they will experiment using a range of grasps as they use different tools to make marks on paper. If very young children are forced to hold a writing tool with the correct grasp before they are developmentally able to do so, their interest and motivation to engage in the writing process can be impaired.

Experiences that support the development of handwriting skills include:

- moulding and squeezing materials such as dough and clay
- finger painting
- finger plays and clapping games
- music and movement
- pasting
- paper tearing
- cutting
- construction toys
- putting together and pulling apart toys and building blocks
- jigsaws
- finger puppets
- ball games
- balancing games
- climbing
- crawling
- negotiating obstacle courses.

There are implications here for the learning environment that we provide for children both indoors and outdoors, as discussed in Chapter 3 (page 20).

Children's early drawings and paintings are associated with the need to represent and experiment with different tools and writing surfaces. Their projection of ideas through drawing and writing processes demonstrates their understanding, thoughts and feelings. As practitioners scribe for children, opportunities are created to model, promote and explore the processes and purposes of handwriting. Young children experiment with and imitate scribbles, shapes, lines, patterns, figures, and letter and numeral shapes. Children enjoy writing signs and messages related to their play, drawing and writing to represent and make meaning. Children will begin to write by imitating the adults they see writing , what they write and how they write, and will produce their own shopping lists, notes, telephone numbers and other messages relevant to their everyday context.

Hill, et al. (2006) refer to the 'sign principle' that develops when children realise that letters and symbols stand for something. Children begin to understand that the drawing of a car represents a car but that the word 'car' has none of the actual features of a car. Hill also refers to the 'linear principle' which is about directionality – young children learn that English is written from left to right in lines that go across the page. Children learn that the same letter can be written in different ways, such as upper case and lower case. Young children need a range of quality materials to experiment with and time and support to practise their emerging handwriting skills. Access to a wide range of books and written texts from different cultures supports their understanding of drawing and writing for different purposes.

How to best support early writing through the use of a writing continuum

Certain aspects of support are relevant to different stages of the writing continuum.

- **Emergence** – immersion in purposeful, relevant learning in writing. Practitioners should surround children with books and environmental print.

- **Demonstration** – an adult modelling writing to show children that writing is purposeful and enjoyable. Practitioners should let children see them writing and provide a wide variety of stimulus and materials for writing.

- **Expectation** – creation of the idea that writing is within the child's grasp. Practitioners should accept and praise what the child does and dwell on their strengths rather than their weaknesses.

- **Responsibility** – the child chooses what and when to write. Practitioners should not present to the child an ordered system of sub-skills. Skills are to be taught when needed to develop child's writing.

- **Approximation** – the child gets close to writing the correct words. Practitioners should allow children to experiment with writing.

- **Employment or practice** – children need to consolidate their skills and understanding of writing. Practitioners should provide many opportunities throughout the day or session for children to engage in writing.

- **Feedback** – young writers need support and encouragement. Practitioners need to provide the correct model without drilling.

Chapter 6
The importance of a secure understanding of child development:
exploring a simple writing continuum

Prerequisite experiences for the support of early writing skills including sensory play have been identified through the work of Alistair Bryce-Clegg (2013) as detailed in his book *Getting Ready To Write*. He lists the following as prerequisites:

- **Wide range of sensory play** – the child enjoys involving the hands; not shying away from involvement in messy play, and is able to tolerate many textures and sensations.

- **Fine finger grasp** – the child can pick up tiny objects between the thumb and index finger easily, but may be faster and more accurate with their dominant hand. When grasping a small object, the thumb and finger form a rounded shape.

- **Controlled release skills** – the child can stack more than ten small blocks using their fingertips.

- **Proximal stability at shoulders, elbows and wrist joints** – the child can support their own weight on their arms when playing 'wheelbarrows', or hang from a monkey bar supporting their own weight, without discomfort. The child can keep shoulders still and relaxed whilst moving their arm and wrist to perform a range of actions.

- **Bilateral use of hands with dominance emerging** – child chooses one hand fairly consistently for activities such as feeding and drawing. When drawing at a table, the child uses both hands, one to hold the pencil and one to stabilise the paper. The child crosses the midline when needed.

- **Use of wrist extension to support the hand when using a pencil** – the child's wrist is slightly extended to enable the fingers to grasp efficiently.

- **Use of a storage grasp and in-hand manipulation skills** – the child is able to hold a small object in their palm with their little and ring fingers, whilst using the index finger and thumb to do something else. The child is able to move small objects from the palm of one hand to the fingertips with increasing ease.

- **Use of a tripod grasp** – the child is able to use this grasp and maintain it while forming shapes.

- **Use of the intrinsic muscles of the hand** – the child is able to use the tiny muscles in the hand to produce the finger movements that are required for highly dextrous activities. These are seen in isolated use when the fingers are spread apart and moved back together, and when the hand forms a pyramid, with fingers straight, on a flat surface.

- **Use of a dynamic tripod grasp** – the child is able to use this grasp and has adequate strength in their fingers and hands to be able to use their hands for prolonged periods without excessive fatigue. This takes years of handwriting practice and fine motor development to mature.

Chapter 6
The importance of a secure understanding of child development:
exploring a simple writing continuum

The following activities will help to build the relevant muscles and prepare children for writing. Try them with very young children to support children's early writing skills.

Finger warm-ups

- **Magic writing gloves** – pull on an imaginary pair of gloves, applying firm pressure to the fingers and back and palm of each hand. (It is a good idea if someone (child or adult) models putting on a pair of real gloves first.) This exercise provides tactile feedback and prepares the muscles for movement.

- **Spider push-ups** – place the fingertips of both hands together and bend and straighten the fingers while pushing the fingertips against each other.

- **Pencil olympics** – twirl a pencil like a baton, spinning it both horizontally and vertically.

- **Wriggle like a snake** – make your fingers wriggle like a snake and, using a tripod grip, move the fingers along the pencil from one end to the other. Use the other hand to hold or support the pencil, then try it without any support.

- **Play the piano** – drum the fingers on a tabletop as if playing a piano. Ensure each fingertip touches the table. Ask children to do it softly and not to drum the fingers too hard.

Upper body warm-ups

Shoulder warm-ups prepare the arm for writing and may help to release tension in the neck and shoulders.

- **Shoulder shrugs** – shrug shoulders forwards, then backwards.

- **Crocodile snaps** – start with one arm straight above the head and the other extended down one side of the body. Snap the hands together meeting above the head, like a crocodile snapping its jaws. Repeat with reversal of arm positions.

- **Controlling the traffic** – start with the elbows bent and the hands in a fist in front of each shoulder. Then straighten the elbows, moving one arm out to the front of the body and the other arm to the side of the body. Alternate the movements.

- **Butterflies** – begin with arms extended straight in front of the body. Link the thumbs to make an 'x' and turn the palms to face out. Using the shoulders to move, make small circles with the hands, moving the hands to the left and right in unison (the fingers lie side by side and are not moving; the movement is coming from the shoulders).

Chapter 6
The importance of a secure understanding of child development:
exploring a simple writing continuum

Introducing the letters of the alphabet in a structured way

Introducing the letters of the alphabet based on the hand and finger movements used to form the letters is particularly helpful for learners with poor fine motor skills. It may be that all of the clockwise letters are not introduced together but in two or more 'groups', interspersed with groups of letters that require a different basic movement. You can also use lengths of tinsel for this.

Possible groupings are:

- the anti-clockwise letters: a d g q c e o s u y f
- the 'stick' letters: i l t j
- the clockwise letters: m n r h p b
- the diagonal letters: k v w x z

If the similarities of movement are pointed out, the children are able to develop a metacognitive awareness of letter formation that can support their letter writing practice.

Letter formations

Teaching correct letter formation involves providing children with opportunities to talk about the names and features of letters and the sounds they represent.

This enhances letter recognition in texts, on computer keyboards and in the environment. When children practise forming letters, they develop a visual and motor memory of their important features.

Looking at the letters and undertaking the movement of writing helps children see and feel how each letter is formed, fixing the letter in the learner's visual memory for future identification and reproduction. The formation of letters involves starting and finishing places, direction of movement and number of strokes per letter. These are important aspects if linking, fluency and speed are to develop with ease. An oval body shape is recommended with a two o'clock starting position for all anti-clockwise ovals.

Chapter 6
The importance of a secure understanding of child development:
exploring a simple writing continuum

Revisiting the *Development Matters* statements

It is worth exploring the *Development Matters* statements on literacy again and considering how these can best be supported having read the previous chapters about creating an environment that truly supports literacy for the 22–36 and 30–50 months stages.

There are many more statements for reading than writing in *Development Matters*, particularly at the 30–50 months stage. The statements for reading are given in Chapter 2 (page 19). The writing statements are shown below:

Writing 22–36 months

- Distinguishes between the different marks they make.

Writing 30–50 months

- Sometimes gives meaning to marks as they draw and paint.

- Ascribes meanings to marks that they see in different places.

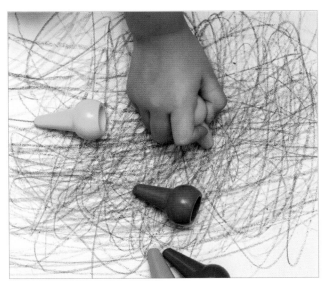

Does this then mean that we should give more attention to reading than mark making or early writing? The answer is no, they both need an equal amount of attention. However, we may see more early progress in reading than in writing at this point in the child's development; although later in their learning journey, as they move into KS1 at school, this will likely change and writing will begin to catch up and often overtake reading.

Chapter 7

Assessing children's early reading and writing – planning the next steps

> Assessment plays an important part in helping parents, carers and practitioners to recognise children's progress, understand their needs, and to plan activities and support.
>
> **DfE, 2017**

There is a saying that 'attitude is everything' (anon). In the area of developing literacy skills, this saying resonates strongly. Children need to develop a real love of books and the desire to create their own books to be able to share their developing and creative ideas. We also have to remember that the Early Learning Goals indicate only the minimum skills, knowledge and understanding in which we need to ensure our children gain competency.

As practitioners we need to be clear about what we are aiming to achieve and how we are likely to do this. In Chapter 1 (page 6), I discussed how children start with experiences which help to move them on to developing their skills and knowledge, and finally this evolves into their conceptual understanding. Some things are easy to measure, and these are often used as statutory performance and development indicators because of this. Other things however, though not as easily measurable, are sometimes equally or even more important, e.g. the emotional wellbeing of children and their attitude towards literacy.

Assessment in literacy

When considering our approach to literacy, we should perhaps be discussing in our settings what we should be trying to measure that we don't already because the *Development Matters* framework doesn't cover it directly (although it might do so indirectly). This might mean further breaking down some of the *Development Matters* statements, particularly where these are more general such as in the earlier stage statements. Doing this will help us

to more clearly identify the next steps for children. This will benefit all children and particularly those children identified with SEND. Assessment should shed light on what children are able to do already, what they are interested in, as well as areas that need further work.

The role of leadership

The role of leadership is to monitor literacy through an overview of assessment of each room across the setting and records of individual children. Supervision is an ideal opportunity for leaders to look at developmental records with key persons and to ensure that developmental assessment records are being suitably completed based on observations made of the children. Any difficulties identified by a key person can be discussed, alongside how the management can support the staff member. Staff should be encouraged to discuss how confident they feel with the assessment process and how they then use the assessments they make to plan the next steps for children.

A child's development journey or profile

A child's development journey or profile is best started by including information from the parents or carers when the child first comes into the setting; this helps to record their starting points. Often this is some form of an 'all about me' record. The key person needs to supplement this with a number of observations of the child during the first few week of starting, so as to accurately assess their stage of development in all areas of learning and development. This will support later identification of the amount of progress made over time in all seven areas.

Summative assessment records should be updated at a minimum of every six to eight weeks, dated or colour-coded to indicate in which half term period they were recorded. Where observational-based summaries of progress are completed, these should include the child's voice and be shared with parents or carers. These should be signed and dated by both the key person and a parent or carer, who should be invited to write or verbally share a comment, which the key person will write on their behalf.

Assessing EAL children

The EYFS requires literacy assessment in English, so practitioners should use all assessment tools, including interpreters where available. It is important to look at all aspects of speech, language and communication development, but within this it is important to gain a picture of home speech, language and communication development by regular dialogue with parents.

Ofsted inspections

Assessment will be a key focus in Ofsted inspections. They will check whether members of staff have a secure understanding of the age group they work with. Linked to this is how assessment information is gathered from observations of children and is informed by parents or carers and previous providers. They will seek to find out how well this observational-based assessment information is then used to plan the next steps and identify any gaps, as well as any children who need additional support. They will make a judgement as to how well this is enabling all children to make good or better progress based on their starting points and identified needs. Recording and assessing children's starting points and learning needs is therefore a key action for key persons and other room staff.

Any assessment should bring about benefits and must be shared with parents and carers. Assessments should be tailored to a specific purpose and should be reliable, valid and fair for that purpose. Indeed, parents can provide valuable assessment information about their child where we support and encourage information sharing. The main purpose of assessment in the EYFS is to support learning, and where appropriate the identification of special needs. Assessments will also give some indication about the quality and effectiveness of the educational programmes we provide.

How we assess

Integral to teaching is how practitioners assess what children know, understand and can do. We also need to take account of the children's individual interests and dispositions to learning (characteristics of effective learning); we use this information to plan children's next steps in learning and monitor their progress.

Development Matters (2012) highlights how observation – the describing of what is taking place through the LOOK, LISTEN and NOTE system – and the formative assessment that follows this fit into the planning cycle. After the observations and assessments have taken place, the question becomes, 'so what?'. How should the adult plan to respond to what they've seen and the assessments they've made? The next steps can be either more of the same – if it is considered that the child needs to consolidate what they know and can do – or the provision of more challenging learning experiences. In reality, the adult will need to carefully consider what they already know about the child and what they have just observed. Any next steps proposed need to spell out in detail:

- what the exact nature of the next steps experience is going to be

- how the learning environment is to be used

- what is required in terms of resources

- the adult role

- when within the routine of the session or day this is going to happen.

The cycle described here starts with practitioners observing the child and noting the significant aspects and then deciding, from these, what children already know and can do which can be taken forward to the next steps.

Formative and summative assessment

Assessment within the EYFS has two facets:

1. formative

2. summative.

Formative assessment

Formative assessment is an ongoing type of assessment that is used to formulate the next steps for children. As such, it is at the heart of good practice every single day. Staff will observe children every day and in every session as they engage in planned activities led by the adult, and in play activities which children initiate and choose themselves. Some will be written down and some will not be. Only that which is significant should be recorded in written form.

However, it is more than just what children do at the setting they attend but also what they do at home with and around parents, carers and siblings that matters. We need to use our partnership with parents to encourage and support them to tell us what their child does at home which demonstrates their growing skills, knowledge and understanding. Partnership and communication with parents is a two-way process; there is the other side of this, namely that we need to share with parents and carers what their child does at the setting. One starting point to further develop this is to consider what opportunities already exist to share information. Once this has been highlighted, we can review how effective these opportunities are and how well they are being used. From this, we can then improve existing arrangements and put in place some additional ones.

Summative assessment

Summative assessment is about recording what children know and can do as part of a summary of their progress. It uses observations to create a summary record of a child's development. Of course, summary assessment records should be regularly shared with parents, but between the ages of 24–36 months, it is a statutory requirement to share a summary with parents – this is also the case at the end of the EYFS through the EYFS profile.

How well assessment works in a setting will depend on the skills of the members of staff. Settings should consider whether some staff training would help to focus and support the desired outcomes.

Within the context of supporting and reviewing or tracking children's progress, both formative and summative assessment are equally important and practitioners need to undertake both of these on a suitably regular basis.

Best fit judgement

Whenever staff members make assessments as to whether a child has achieved a stage or part of a stage, this has to be made on the basis of what is called a 'best fit' judgement. What this means is that based on the evidence available, including key person knowledge of the child, on the balance of this evidence, it is a sound decision to judge that the child has achieved a certain goal or level because this fits best with what is known about the child.

Making best fit judgements which are accurate and sound takes a certain level of knowledge and understanding, gained through experience and training. Staff who do not feel as confident or competent to make best fit judgements will benefit from coaching support from more experienced colleagues around them or a training course. In the case of a childminder, this may be someone working in another setting – either a day nursery, another childminder, a children's centre or a linked local school.

Moderation of the accuracy of summary assessment

It is vitally important that the assessments made about children are accurate, otherwise:

- the next steps planned will not be appropriate or suitable

- children moving onto the next stage of their learning (either to another room in a setting, or to another setting, including school) will not have their needs suitably met right from the start because the main teaching provided will be based on the assessments passed on at the point of transition.

In conclusion, it's about the environment, the routines of the day and the role that adults take up that make the real impact in inspiring children towards becoming literate. All of the above supports the observation, assessment and planning processes that are so important in maximising children's progress.

Bibliography and further reading

Athey, C. (2007) *Extending Thought in Young Children: A Parent – Teacher Partnership.* (revised edition). Sage Publications

Bryce-Clegg, A. (2013), *Getting Ready to Write: Improving Provision and Outcomes for the Children in Your Setting.* Featherstone

Clay, M. M. (1991), *Becoming literate: The Construction of Inner Control.* Heinemann.

DfE (2016), *Early Years Foundation Stage Profile Results in England*, 2016. Crown copyright

DfE (2017), *Statutory Framework for the Early Years Foundation Stage: Setting the Standards for Learning, Development and Care for Children From Birth to Five.* Crown copyright

DCSF The National Strategies Early Years (2008), *Mark making Matters: Young Children Making Meaning in All Areas of Learning and Development.* Crown copyright

Dombey, H. et al. (1998), *Whole to Part Phonics: How Children Learn to Read and Spell.* Heinemann

Early Education (2012), *Development Matters in the Early Years Foundation Stage (EYFS).* Crown copyright

Golomb, C. (1981), 'Representations and reality: The origins and determinants of young children's drawing' in *Review of Research in Visual Art Education*, pp. 247–266

Gould, T. (2013), *Learning and Playing Outdoors: How to plan and create an inspring outdoor environment.* Featherstone

Gould, T. (2013), *Press It, Switch It, Turn it, Move it! Providing High Quality Early ICT Experiences.* Featherstone

Gould, T. (2012), *Learning and Playing Indoors: How to Create an Inspiring Indoor Environment.* Featherstone

Gould, T. (2011), *Effective Practice in Outdoor Learning: If in Doubt, Let Them Out!* Featherstone

Gould, T. (2008), '*Laying Sound Foundations for Literacy*'. In *English 4 to11*, pp. 6–10

Gould, T. (2003), '*Children's Literacy Development at the Foundation Stage*'. In *English 4 to 11*, pp. 21–25

Gould, T. Brierly, J. and Coates-Mohammed, K. (2012), *Learning and Playing Indoors: How to Create an Inspiring Indoor Environment.* Featherstone

Hill, P. et al. (2006), *Breakthrough* Corwin Press

Hymes, D. H. (1963), *Essays in the History of Linguistic Anthropology* University of Pensylvania

Kellogg, R. (1970), *Analysing Children's Art.* Palo Alto California

Malchiodi C. A. (1998), *Understanding Children's Drawings.* London: Jessica Kingsley

Matthews, J. (1992), 'The genesis of aesthetic sensibility' in Thistlewood, D. (ed.) *Drawing Research and Development*, NSEAD and Longman, pp. 26–33

Matthews, J. (1999), *The Art of Childhood and Adolescence: The Construction of Meaning.* London: Falmer Press

Morgan, N. (2015), *Why knowledge matters*, DfE

Nutbrown, C. (1996), *Respectful Educators – Capable Learners: Children's Rights and Early Education.* Sage Publications

Ofsted (2015), The Common Inspection Framework: *Education, Skills and Early Years.* Crown copyright

Ofsted (2015), Early Years Inspection Handbook: *Handbook for Inspecting Early Years in England Under Sections 49 and 50 of the Childcare Act 2006.* Crown Copyright

Palmer, S. and Bayley, R. (2013), *Foundations of Literacy: A Balanced Approach to Language, Listening and Literacy Skills in the Early Years* (revised edition). Featherstone

Rich, D. (2002), *More Than Words: children developing communication, language and literacy.* Early Education

Vygotsky, L. S. (1995), *Imagination and Creativity in Childhood.* Gothenburg: Daidalos